BUSINESS WAR GAMES

How Large, Small, and New Companies Can Vastly Improve Their Strategies and Outmaneuver the Competition

By
Benjamin Gilad, PhD

CAREER PRESS
Franklin Lakes, NJ

Business War Games
Edited by Jodi L. Brandon
Typeset by Eileen Dow Munson
Cover design by The Design Works Group
Printed in the U.S.A. by Book-mart Press

To order this title, please call toll-free 1-800-CAREER-1 (NJ and Canada: 201-848-0310) to order using VISA or MasterCard, or for further information on books from Career Press.

CAREER PRESS

The Career Press, Inc., 3 Tice Road, PO Box 687,
Franklin Lakes, NJ 07417

www.careerpress.com

Library of Congress Cataloging-in-Publication Data

Gilad, Benjamin.

Business war games : how large, small, and new companies can vastly improve their strategies and outmaneuver the competition / by Benjamin Gilad.

p. cm.

Includes index.

ISBN 978-1-60163-030-8

1. Management games. 2. War games. 3. Strategic planning—Simulation methods. 4. Management—simulation methods. I. Title.

HD30.26.G55 2009
658.4'012--dc22

2008021195

Dedication

To my loved ones,
Shirly, Corinne, and Milo.

And to my parents,
Arye and Hilda,
who raised me to battle for my ideas.

Acknowledgments

Many people contributed their time and experience to this book. Michael Sperger of SAP (and formerly of IBM) contributed his superb writing style, sense of humor and irony, and knowledge of world history to Chapter 2. I wanted him to co-author the whole book with me, but he had other, unexplained priorities, such as feeding his family. David Hartman, of *StrategicSurprise.com*, a unique strategy consultancy, contributed his knowledge of Israeli military war games to Chapter 2, and reviewed many of the earlier drafts of this book, which he inexplicably liked. Deni Deasy sharply focused the message of this book with her very astute changes.

Helen Ho of Telus, the Canadian Telcom company, and Matthew Morgan, a McKinsey consultant who at the time was an MBA student at Harvard Business School, contributed the case research to Chapter 12 on strategic junctions. They worked out of their love of research and the challenge of proving that hindsight is valuable. I am forever grateful.

Pat McGraw, a student of mine at the Academy of Competitive Intelligence, wrote a paper while doing his MBA studies, based on my concept of hindsight intelligence research, and was gracious enough to allow me to use it for Chapter 12. His faculty supervisor, incidentally, thought the subject was inappropriate for his MBA thesis....

My agent, Jackie Meyer, of Whimsy Literary Agency in New York City, is a unique individual. She believed in this book from the start, and worked tirelessly to promote it. She never wavered and never lost faith, even as she had to listen to my black-and-white worldview while sedated from a dental treatment. Thanks, Jackie.

Michael Pye, of Career Press, was enthusiastic from day one. He never took offense, even as I tried to convince him I knew more about how this book needed to look than his company, with its proven formula for success.

Jodi Brandon, my editor at Career Press was a delight to work with. Not once did she complain about my English being my second (or maybe third) language, which meant a lot of syntax and grammer inventions on my part.

Elizabeth Barndollar contributed several amazin illustrations to this book. Alas, the format allows for only partial view of her talent.

Finally, many corporate intelligence managers contributed heavily to this book without knowing it at the time. To all my friends who invited me to run war games at their companies, risking their careers and reputations, I thank you from the bottom of my heart.

A special note goes to Dr. Gary Costley, former CEO of Kellogg USA, and later Chairman and CEO of Multifoods Corporation; Carlos Gutierrez, former VP Marketing for Kellogg USA, later Kellogg Corp.'s Chairman and CEO, and now Secretary of Commerce in the Bush Administration; Jeff Webster, former Director of CI for Kellogg, now Senior Vice President of Tyson Foods, and General Manager of its Renewable Products Division; and Celeste Clarke, Senior Vice President for Global Nutrition and Corporate Affairs, Kellogg Corp. Your talents and hard work may have helped you reach your esteemed positions, but let's focus on the truly important factor: You were the first to play my war game! See how far it got you? I am forever in your debt for believing in me.

Contents

Foreword

In March 2003, Cadbury Schweppes closed its biggest acquisition ever: the purchase of the Adams Company from Pfizer for $4.2 billion.

With Adams came great brands such as Trident, Halls, Dentyne, Chiclets, Clorets, and Certs—and, as the second-largest chewing gum company in the world, the right to compete against Wrigley, the global number one in gum.

Adams had not distinguished itself from an operating perspective in the years before our acquisition. Its revenue was flat. Margins had dropped from 19 percent to 12 percent, and it had lost share to Wrigley on a global basis and in its largest market, the United States, for several years due to a stream of Wrigley innovation.

The financial markets were unhappy with what they viewed as an expensive acquisition, a complex integration, and an inexperienced team led by an equally inexperienced leader: me. They were also convinced we would be unable to compete with Wrigley. Not surprisingly, our share price fell by almost 30 percent!

Clearly, we needed to demonstrate strong commercial and financial results quickly if we were to earn the market's respect and restore our share price decline. Believing that financial results follow commercial results, we sought to validate our acquisition model, which required an average of 7-percent revenue growth across both contested markets and uncontested markets to deliver a return to high teens margins for the Adams business.

As a significant element of this validation process, we needed to conduct an analysis of "where to play and how to win"—or, in other words, where and how to best deploy our innovation and commercial resources against markets and competitors to the greatest effect. After a thorough search, we retained Ben Gilad to lead us through such an analysis.

The event, which was conducted as a "war game," was engaging, revealing, and fun. It took place over three days in the usual business hotel, where our top 50–60 business leaders responsible for delivery of the acquisition case smoked their own exhaust under Ben's incisive leadership. The result was our first global gum strategy.

The numbers speak for themselves. We beat our acquisition case covering the cost of capital a year early. By 2007, Adams' core brands had grown more than 7 percent per annum, and margins had returned to 19 percent; Trident sales had almost doubled, making it the largest gum brand in the world; Adams' gum share in the United States had grown from 25 percent to 34 percent (while Wrigley's has declined from 62 percent to 58 percent); and globally Cadbury's gum share had grown from 7 percent to 27 percent (while Wrigley's remained flat at 34 percent). Over the 2004–2007 period, our Total Shareowner Return, or TSR, averaged more than 20 percent, driven by a share price that quickly recovered the 30-percent initial loss and moved on to new heights.

From my perspective, these accomplishments reflect the focus and effort of a great team of people across multiple fronts informed by an outstanding "war games" process of business and financial self-analysis led by Ben.

Enjoy the book and the battle!

Todd Stitzer

CEO, Cadbury

London, March 2008

Part I

From Sand Table to Boardroom

Chapter 1

War Gaming Made *Simple*

War games in business are ***hot.***

Recent reports in the business press suggest the large consulting firms are running three times the war games they used to just a few years ago.

Yet, chances are, if you are not a senior executive, you have not been invited to them. The typical war game in a large corporation is a large-scale, expensive exercise, with sophisticated computer modeling, a small army of consultants from a big consulting firm, and days of preparations and data inputting. These games are mostly restricted to top executives and their advisors.

That makes no sense. War games do not need to be expensive, nor do they require a prestigious consulting firm. Further, the experience and results should be accessible to every manager in the corporate world who faces decisions involving competitors; they should not be just for top executives.

More than anything, though, war games should be *realistic.*

They should bring practical ideas to help you make better decisions and plans that can survive market reaction.

You should be able to use war games to replace "naval gazing" with a more insightful, external perspective of your markets and your products.

Marketing managers, brand teams, and product and project leaders should be able to run quick, cheap, and effective war games to:

- Assess and anticipate changes in their markets.
- Pressure-test global and regional strategies.
- Develop and test plans to go after existing competitors or defend against rising threats.
- "Insulate" new launches.
- Get a buy-in, identify gaps in market knowledge, and create a defensible business case.

This is what this manual is all about: I intend to teach you *step-by-step* how to organize, prepare, and run your war game with your team at a fraction of the cost of the big consultants.

Reading this book may just mean the difference between your plan reaching its goals or crashing out there.

What Are War Games?

More than 2,000 years ago, the Battle of Cannae pitched 72,000 legionnaires from the almighty Roman Empire against 32,000 tribesmen under Hannibal of the tiny city-state Carthage. If you follow the diagrams, you will see, move after move, how Hannibal won that famous battle.

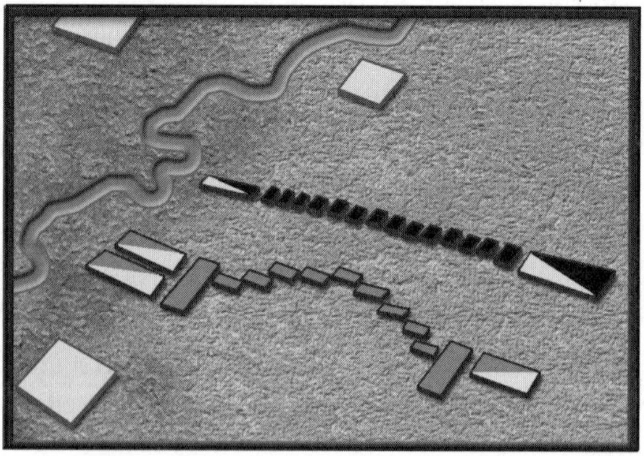

The previous diagram depicts the initial positions. The Roman forces are on top. Both armies placed their infantry in the center, with a cavalry unit on each side. Note that Hannibal's left cavalry wing was much larger than the right, and that his center was pitched forward.

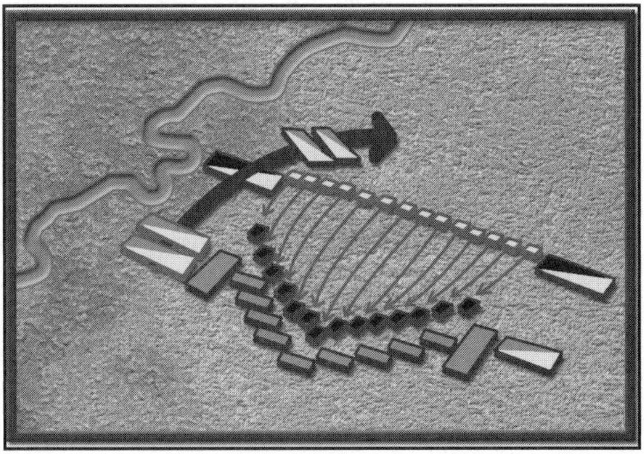

Because they enjoyed tremendous numerical superiority, the Romans attacked first, sending in their infantry. Hannibal knew that was what they were likely to do. He ordered his center to retreat and, at the same time, the large left-wing cavalry to start a flanking maneuver, overwhelming the numerically inferior Roman cavalry wing.

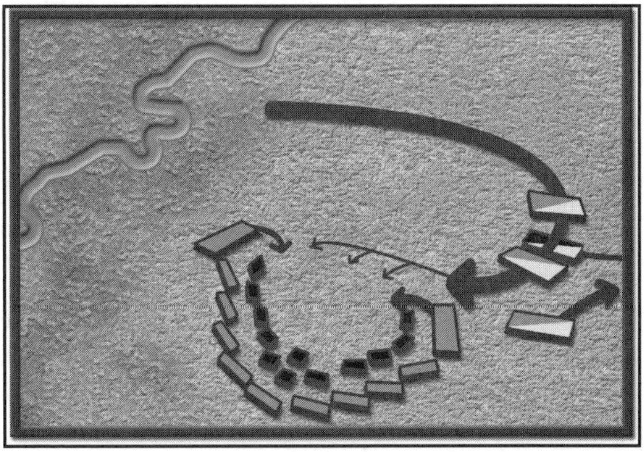

In the heat of the advance, the Romans did not notice that they were being flanked from behind, and that Hannibal's infantry was drawing them into an arc. Then Hannibal's center stopped retreating.

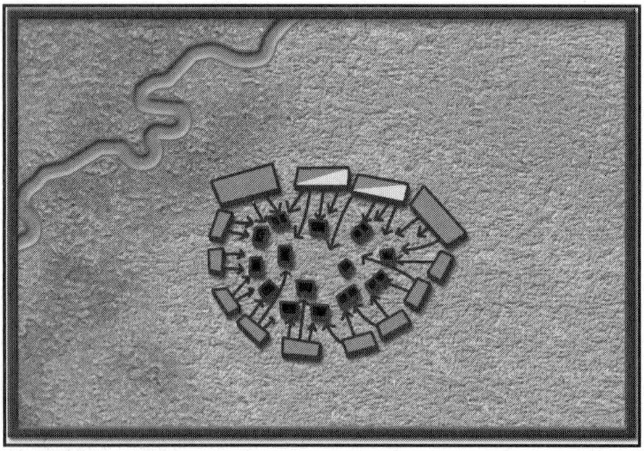

The Roman legionnaires were surrounded. Sixty thousand of them perished that day, making it one of the bloodiest battles in the history of wars.

These four short reenactment visuals tell a tale of superior planning by Hannibal. He figured out the Roman initial positions, their first move, and their responses (or lack thereof) to his countermoves. We can imagine him standing on a hill, under the hot Italian sun (it was August), surrounded by his generals, drawing the battle plan in the sand: "I *know* the Romans. This is what they will do, and then when we do that, they will move here, and you, Hasdrubal, then take the cavalry and...."

Fast-forward 2000 years. Abstract from generals and sand tables (and later toy soldiers or red paint guns), what is the *unique essence* of war gaming? After a bit of thought you realize the principle:

War gaming is nothing more than role-playing in order to understand a third party, with the goal of answering: What *will* the opponent do? What then is my *best* option?

We all role-play various third parties throughout our lives, in order to understand their perspectives. We try to think the way our boss does, in order to improve our odds of gaining his approval for our ideas; we try to put ourselves in the shoes of our teenagers ("I was young once, too, you know?"), in order to be able to relate better to them. And when we say in exasperation: "What were you *thinking*?" we actually admit a failure of insight into another person's perspective.

War Gaming in Business: Where Does It Make the Most Sense?

If war gaming is about external perspective and insight *through* role-playing opponents, where would it make most sense in business? The answer is, clearly, in testing a competitive plan—for a single product, a brand portfolio, a division, or a whole company. Why is role-playing such powerful a tool for competitive planning? The chance of success for any and every competitive strategy depends to a large degree on the reactions of *third parties* such as competitors, but, because most of us do not have *direct* knowledge of these intended reactions, role-playing allows us to predict these reactions without such knowledge.

The "We've Already Taken This Into Account" Myth

In *The Halo Effect* (Free Press, 2007), an intriguing and thoughtful book written by Professor Phil Rosenzweig of the IMD school in Lausanne, Switzerland, the author exposes the flawed assumption behind best-selling books promoting a "formula for success" (such as *Build to Last*, *From Good to Great*, *What Really Works*, and *In Search of Excellence*) and much-hyped studies of corporate performance by such prestigious consulting firms as McKinsey & Co., and Bain, who claim to have identified the definitive set of behaviors and characteristics leading to the high performance of successful companies. One of the most persistent fallacies of those studies involved what he terms "The Delusion of Absolute Performance," in which companies are told by the gurus and consultants that their success depends largely, if not solely, on their own actions, as if performance was absolute. In Rosenzweig's words:

> The Delusion of Absolute Performance is hugely important because it suggests that companies can achieve high performance by following a simple formula, regardless of the actions of competitors. [McKinsey's] Evergreen Project wasn't alone in this basic misconception—the same delusion was implicit in Build to Last, where [authors] Collins and Porras claimed that following a handful of steps provided a "blueprint for enduring success" without any mentioning of rivals or any appreciation of the dynamic of industry competition. Yet *once you see that performance is relative, it becomes obvious that companies can never achieve success simply by following a given set of steps, no matter how well intended; their success will always be affected by what rivals do.*[1] (italics added)

It is a natural attitude of managers to believe that success depends on their own hard work and smarts, and that their plans already account for competitors' likely actions. However, this bias towards an optimistic attitude causes the vast majority of managers to pay lip service to others' actions. Instead, they should consider their plans as bets that come with risk, a risk originating from competitive dynamics in their markets, and study those risks carefully to minimize them. War gaming will not guarantee their success—nothing will—but it will *increase the odds in their favor.*

War Games Without Computers

Did Hannibal need a laptop? No. Superior plans have nothing to do with computer simulations. Unfortunately, computer simulations have been popular features of war gaming in the military and with big consulting firms and big-budget games.

"I'd like to run our market domination forecast once more, but, this time, let's see what happens if we plug evil flying monkeys into the equation."

They are unnecessary. They make games expensive. You want an *inexpensive*, *quick*, *simple*, and *realistic* war gaming methodology, a methodology you can apply to decisions *all over the company*. When it comes to predicting competitors' behavior, computer algorithms are especially short on the realism part. This manual is about role-playing using analytical and behavioral models, which are much more powerful than software programs; trying to understand the *motivation* of a competitor is both cheaper and more effective than an army of consultants running algorithms in the back room.

Why Not Game Theory?

Some consulting firms in recent years offer war games based on game theory programming. Game theory is a mathematical branch of economics that models interactions between non-cooperative multiple parties. However, despite game theorists' proclamations, game theory applicability to strategic plans is severely limited. Game theoretic simulations that promise to find "optimal" or "stable" solutions in a world of suboptimal decision-makers and dynamic competition fail to meet the criteria of simple, transparent, and *realistic* games. Their predictions of stable solutions are not consistent with observed behavior. Their resultant moves fail to meet Michael Porter's criterion of superior strategy, which has little to do with equilibrium solutions among millions of possibilities, and everything to do with distinctive activities. (There's more about game theory and other mathematical modeling of market behavior in the appendix to Chapter 4.) The good news is that there are other inexpensive, fun, and simple methods that bring more realism into your plans and at the same time save a bundle!

Humans Make It Realistic

Based on my experience with both human and computer-based games, role-playing games bring far superior results, because predicting human and organizational behavior is far beyond current mathematical models. Role-playing war games focus on understanding market perspective, leading to insight about differentiation as a basis for superior strategy, not on generic solutions. Finally, because role-playing games are transparent and simple, they are easily accessible. They can therefore improve plans and strategies *at all levels of the organization*.

War Games Without the War?

War gaming is about role-playing. Still, the term implies war. There are some managers who get turned on and others who get turned off by the origin of the term *war games* with the military. Many businesses may be locked in a "heated battle" for customers, but that's as far as the analogy with war should go. Though the origin of war games may be in the military, business is much more difficult and much more complex subject than war. There is a reason why, in the United States, entrepreneurs are heroes and inspiration models, where generals are, well, generally *not*. There is little concrete value business managers can derive from military war game techniques. In business, strategy is always about a third party (the customer) whose role in deciding who is a "victor" is rather complex and may involve keeping the competition alive rather than allowing for a decisive "victory." There are signs that military planners are actually learning this lesson from business. The changing strategy of U.S. forces in Iraq in late 2007, which enlisted the cooperation of the purported "customers" (the Sunni population) to fight Al Qaeda, showed a beginning of an understanding of this complexity.

So, though at times we may use analogies such as the "battlefield," we adamantly *refuse* to quote clichés from Sun Tzu's book *The Art of War*. Clichés affect mindsets, and mindsets affect thinking. One needs a sense of appreciation and shared values to try and understand the other side's *logic* and actions. The Japanese had that mentality down to an art, which made it easier for them to compete. They admired the big American firms, and then set out to defeat—oops, sorry, to take away market leadership from—them.

Would You Prefer "IRS"?

So, if war games are not about wars, and not about computer games, why use the term? There are several much more appropriate terms such as "What Will Go Wrong Exercise" (WWGWE), "Competitor Role-Playing Workshop" (CRPW), "Strategy Dry-Run Test" (SDRT), or my favorite: "Iterations of Rivals' Strategies" (IRS). Not very appealing, are they? "War game" *sounds* fun, and one of the most important qualities of war gaming is that it has to be fun to accomplish its objectives. In a corporate culture where fun is typically reserved to the Christmas party, war gaming is a refreshing change.

So with your permission, we'll keep the term, and you keep remembering it is not about war and it is not about fantasy games.

So What Is the Best Way to War Game?

Since the ancient Greek days, acting has been the art of role-playing characters. According to legendary acting teacher Stella Adler, "The actor's job is to defictionalize the fiction."[2] The actor must live within the fictional character as if it is real. The same basic principle applies to business war games: Teams have to live within the competitors' reality as if they were their competitor. Getting to *think* like the character (in this case, the competitor they role-play) allows managers to make accurate predictions about competitors' real moves.

No, I'm not suggesting you take acting lessons and go to auditions. But I do suggest you learn to put together a competitor's *character*.

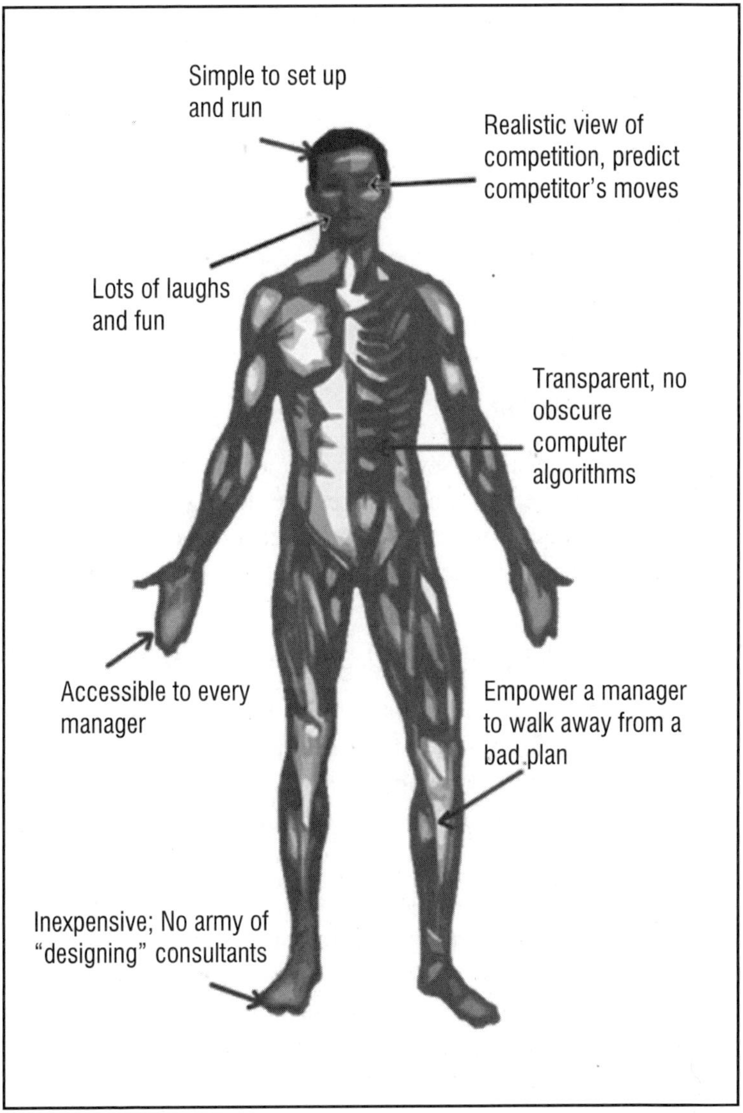
Simple to set up
and run
Realistic view of
competition, predict
competitor's moves
Lots of laughs
and fun
Transparent, no
obscure
computer
algorithms
Accessible to every
manager
Empower a manager
to walk away from a
bad plan
Inexpensive; No army of
"designing" consultants

The seven tests of an effective war game.

The 7 Tests of Effective War Gaming

It has to be:

1. Realistic.
2. Empowering.
3. Accessible.
4. Lots of fun.
5. Inexpensive.
6. Simple.
7. Transparent.

To remember these seven tests, remember this simple acronym: An effective war game makes the manager a **REALIST.** Effective managers are neither optimistic nor pessimistic. They meet the market reality well prepared.

Aren't Most Managers Already Realists?

Maybe you are, but many are not. Larry Bossidy and Ram Charan, one a highly respected former Chairman and CEO of Honeywell-Allied-Signal, and the other an accomplished academic, reveal in their book *Confronting Reality* (Crown Publishing, 2004):

> In theory, confronting reality is what business is all about. More than most, businesspeople like to think they're realists. Their actions look like realism: They work hard to gather relevant facts and data, they research alternatives rigorously, and they bring their cumulative knowledge and experience to bear on the issues. They test their thinking. Then they reach conclusions. But those conclusions are all too often unjustified. Unless you're in a rare organization, you've seen this yourself. In our decades of experience, we've

wrestled firsthand with it in hundreds of companies and many industries. The best strategies, the most rigorous research, the clearest of operating plans—all are undermined because *the key people behind them have missed the reality of the situation for one reason or another.*[3] (italics added)

When to Play a War Game

War games are not a panacea. They must be played for the right reasons. Here are the three obvious prerequisites:

Formal Prerequisites for a War Game

1. You need to make a decision, create a plan.
2. There are external third parties whose reactions greatly affect the success of this decision, and you do not have direct intelligence on their intended reactions, nor are they inclined to provide you with an advanced copy of their plans.
3. There is cost involved if your decision is a *wrong* one.

These three necessary conditions are not sufficient, though.

When Not to Play War Games

War gaming is not for everyone, and not for every occasion. There are two additional prerequisites, the absence of which can make war games rather useless (even if the situation meets the three formal prerequisites).

Informal Prerequisites for a War Game

1. Management allows for the possibility of plans to go wrong, and is willing to make changes to strategy to improve its odds under competitive pressure.

2. Management allows a free exchange of information in a game.

If your boss already made up his mind about a strategy, there is little point in running a game.

"It's quite a sophisticated machine. It can shred paper, plastic, cardboard, big egos, bad attitudes, and fear!"

A recent *USA Today* article (Jan. 16, 2007) reported that the median score of CEOs' ability to accept criticism was significantly lower than any other level in their organizations. If an executive is unable to admit mistakes, or look critically at his own strategy, a war game will not result in empowerment to walk away from a bad plan (failing Test 2 of the 7 Tests of Effective War Gaming). George Jones, Border's CEO, is quoted in that article as saying: "People tend to overpraise [sic] the CEO's ideas, overlooking their flawed logic, or unsupported assumptions."[4] Jones made it clear to *his* 28,000 employees that he was not looking to surround himself with "yes people."

He is an example of a good potential sponsor of a war game. However, some executives are narcissistic, and see their plans as infallible. It does not mean they have bad strategies. They simply cannot make good use of war gaming. I would not run a war game with either Lee Iacocca or Dick Cheney in the room.

The prerequisite of free information flow is more subtle. I've been involved in war games where management tried to restrict the information available to the participants, or the topics to be addressed, or even the legal boundaries of the discussion. A company might be embroiled in anti-trust litigation, and its lawyers may be leery of *any* discussion of competition (this is not a hypothetical example); or management might be involved in high-level merger discussions that it keeps under tight wraps, and the results of a war game may become moot. A game may touch on sensitive corporate taboos, and your boss may ask that those elephants be left outside the room. A war game that runs into these issues is no longer simple to run and therefore at risk of failing Test 6 (Simple). Be sure before you embark on this exercise that it is indeed straightforward: What *will* competitors do? What is my *best* strategy given their moves?

War Gaming and the More Traditional Planning Approaches

War gaming does not replace strategic planning. It is a technique to be used with traditional planning processes. When it comes to evaluating strategies in light of likely reactions from opponents, war gaming is the most focused on the external perspectives and therefore effective in getting one away from rehashing internal beliefs. As far as the ubiquitous discounted cash flow models are concerned, war games make the assumptions underlying them at least *semi*-realistic.

If you adhere to this clear space of gaining deeper understanding of market players' perspectives, where war gaming beats any other method, you will find the exercise enormously beneficial.

"We're devoting two years to develop a five year plan to revise our three year plan for the implementation of our ten year plan."

Fringe Benefits of Effective War Games

(*There's no need to read this section if you are already a convert!)

Sustained External Focus

War games are effective in externalizing the focus of management teams in need of less naval gazing beyond the game itself. In some companies, following a war game, managers continued to track their assigned parties for years to verify which of their predictions came true.

Intelligence Gaps

War games help discover problematic intelligence gaps. Questions such as "what do we know?" and "what more do we need to know?" are quickly answered in a single war game, whether this was *or was not* one of its stated objective. Organizations live and die by how much they know about their markets, which includes understanding other players. The list of other players is long. It starts with customers; those who have never been customers, preferring to buy from competitors; those who have been customers but have since moved to buying from competitors; those who never bought products from the industry incumbents. It then goes to competitors/new competitors, those who'll become competitors if they get funding; suppliers, and those who can become suppliers (outsourcing); regulatory and other influencing agencies; distributors; and many other players that create the balance of power in the industry.

We call the total *sum* of that intimate knowledge competitive intelligence. To be successful in the long run, a company needs to collectively assemble deep and expansive competitive intelligence—as in knowledge of what matters and what does not in its market. This intelligence is gathered by numerous individuals and units inside the company as a matter of course, but a lot of it is implicit, stored in departmental silos, and hardly shared across units. Many organizations actually lack basic knowledge of what they *know*. It is not a surprise, therefore, that few organizations have a clear notion of what they *do not know*. Significant holes in market or industry intelligence (ignoring a new entrant, lack of timely knowledge of a shift in customers' preferences or needs, failure to recognize the significance of a regulatory/political move by interest groups) can bring down an organization or an executive or a whole industry in amazingly short time. Think Fannie Mae. Think Polaroid. Think Ford. Think fixed-line telephony.

A war game, by nature, is run on intelligence—how else would you role-play competitors?—and therefore allows immediate feedback on what intelligence is missing. Not all holes can be plugged (at least not legally); competitors or potential competitors' development plans, for example, are not legally obtainable. But other holes become obvious and are eye-openers: "We don't truly know why our competitor is making money in China." "We actually have no clue what customers think are our own *strengths*." These are real statements from war games. War games drive knowledge searching as often as they drive strategic thinking.

Buy-In

War games create buy-in in two ways. First, war games expose quite clearly gaps in management communication. In a war game at a biotech company aimed at launching a new drug, management concluded that the most important aspect of the game was the realization that managers in the company did not clearly know what the company stood for. The launch plan had lower odds of succeeding without a clearer sense of how management saw the place of that drug in its whole portfolio, as this drug positioning could not be done in a vacuum.

That biotech company was not unique. The majority of the large companies with which I have worked suffered from some form of communication breakdown over management strategy. In my 20 years of running war games around the globe, I can recall maybe 20 percent of the Fortune 500 companies whose mid-managers did not complain about top executives' visions being muddy, being kept close to their chests, never being fully elaborated on, and so forth. Quite often, strategy is communicated in slogans that have more to do with goals than strategy. ("We will retain our leadership by being the leader in innovation" is not a strategy; it's a sound bite.) A war game puts strategy on the table, not always in a flattering way. However, at the end of a day testing the assumptions underlying it, putting competitors' perspectives around it, your strategy becomes real. Simultaneously, you create the foundation of buy-in, which goes a long way towards drawing support for a plan.

Self-Awareness

What are our true strengths? What are our weaknesses? These are worthy questions a business manager grapples with daily. The traditional technique to answering these questions is to run a SWOT exercise (Strengths, Weaknesses, Opportunities, and Threats). It should stand instead for Silly Way Of Thinking. Knowing your true strengths implies an objective comparison with competitors' capabilities, which is rare in most organizations. Identifying weaknesses implies an honest, apolitical distribution of "blame," at best a difficult issue in most organizations. And then there are those blind spots: weaknesses that are unknown to you, but known to the market.

Take, for example, the pharmaceutical industry. It is very successful on average, but its good fortunes are under increasing attack. Pharma faces more third-party participants tagging at its heels than a senator in a lobbyists' convention. The reactions and actions of the following multitudes of constituencies make a huge impact on the success of failure of new drugs: physicians, key opinion leaders (important physicians), hospitals, medical benefit administrators, purchasing groups, patients, patients associations, insurers, HMOs, employers, public payers (governments), regulators, and competitors. Yet large pharmaceutical companies have been employing the same business model for the past 25 years or so, underestimating significant shifts among those external crowds. The business model fundamentals include a huge upfront investment in trial-and-error discovery process, reminiscent of a lottery, a hugely expensive clinical testing process governed by an inefficient government body (FDA), and then throwing more and more salespeople (clinical "detailers") at the same set of doctors with a shrinking attention span, until they reach a spectacularly declining productivity curve. When all that fails, companies buy other companies or license their compounds, in the hope of recharging a drying pipeline. Acquiring promising new products, they will then try to sell them with more and more salespeople, and less and less cooperative doctors, as well as more and more reluctant payers and suspicious patients.

Does this picture seem right? How long do pharmaceutical companies think they can keep up this model in light of public opinion, political sensitivities, increasing payer power, and doctors' disdain? When the model breaks down, as it has started to do, a company can find itself on the hot seat faster than one can say Hillary Clinton. Case in point: Pfizer, who in 2007 ousted its Chairman and CEO and appointed its first outsider to the helm to try and reverse a rapidly declining fortune. The bit of self awareness and self examination brought about through war games *may* do many pharma executives a lot of good, even if it starts at a single product level.

Case Study

There's a New Sheriff in Town

Ed Lasky (not his real name) has been recently appointed president of the Industrial Machinery division of Henderson & Co. (not its real name), an icon of American high-tech industrial manufacturing.

Ed was flattered, excited, and a little bit anxious. He would have been insane not to have been a bit anxious. The division had a strong free cash flow for the previous three years, but its future was regarded as cloudy. The familiar saying "the past does not predict the future" applied perfectly to this old fashioned company. From the leading manufacturer of its products in the global market in the 1980s, the division slipped to number three in its industry at present time. Most of its cash emanated from servicing existing installations, and its share in selling new products had been lost to European and Asian competitors. The division was at a very real crossroad.

Ed was facing the need to formulate *new* and viable strategy for this division, as its current strategy ran out of steam. He chose to run a war game.

Why did Ed choose a war game? Talking to him, I found his reasoning both riveting and informative of the way new leaders approach their challenges. He faced the need to build a strong case to the parent company for the future of the division, and build consensus among his managers for this business case, or the division might end up with a "For Sale" sign on its door and he would lose his job. He felt that both time and an accurate reading of the competitive situation were simultaneously of essence to him.

Let us sum up Ed's situation again, because so many managers can find themselves in a similar state on their way *up*. He needed to:

1. Formulate a ***better*** strategy.
2. Build a strong ***business*** case behind this strategy.
3. Get a ***buy-in*** from key people.

We can call it the "3b" case for short.

The 3b Case as a Special Case of War Gaming

A 3b case is quite a familiar situation for a new leader, whether it is at a company level, a division, a country, a brand or a product team. The 3b case carries with it a challenge that is quite daunting: In order to formulate a strategy with a real chance of success (that is, a strategy built on clear assessment of market reactions), a new leader needs to get an accurate assessment of the various other players in the market, and their potential actions and reactions. *Strategies that are created in a vacuum, succeed in a vacuum only.*

In order to get an accurate assessment of other players' likely moves and countermoves, a new leader needs to identify the parties inside or outside his organization who actually possess that rare knowledge, and get them to share their knowledge with him in a short time.

Neither task is simple or straightforward.

Ed knew he could hire a management consulting firm to help with assessing competitors' capabilities and responses and deliver the strategic advice. However, he was weary of their strong biases and inflexible doctrines. He had a good reason to be weary. As Michael Porter points out in his seminal book, *Competitive Strategy* (Free Press, 1980), knowing who your competitor's *habitual* consultant is, is one good starting point to predicting its moves.

Ed was going to talk to his executives, naturally. However, he was very mindful of the risk of tapping them exclusively. In that, he followed many new leaders. In a March 29, 2006 interview in *Fortune* magazine, the legendary new CEO of JP MorganChase, Jamie Dimon was quoted saying, "In a big company, it's easy for people to b.s. you. A lot of them have been practicing for decades."[5] The old guard would fiercely defend the forte, and then there would be those who blamed the previous management for everything including global warming and the rise of sunspots. Big egos and the politics of power at the top echelon of companies exclude an objective assessment of the competitive situation. A lot of good knowledge of the competitive reality resides with *middle management and field people*, not top management, according to Ed.

The vexing problem of how to get to the people with the objective external knowledge and how to know that what they tell *is* objective ranks up there as one of the most challenging tasks facing any new leader. In an unstructured discussion process between the new leader and his people, the boss is more likely to get his ear filled with complaints about internal problems than good input about the market's reality. Moreover, the prerogative of slowly and patiently traversing the landscape in search of understanding is reserved for monks and the heirs of large private fortunes, not executives under time pressure. Ed wanted a quicker way, and war gaming presented him with an effective alternative.

The way Ed looked at it, a war game was a unique setting for sharing expertise: structured, constructive, and relatively safe. The reason middle managers would feel relatively "safe" in a war game, he suggested, is because a war game legitimizes the poking of "holes" and airing of blind spots in a company's strategy through the potential actions of *rivals*. The best argument for doing that freely is that, if they do not, competitors *will*. At the same time, by using role-playing to get "in character," war games optimize the use of limited information to make the best predictions regarding competitors' and potential competitors' intentions. With a war game behind him, Ed reasoned, he could form his own view of the market and the best strategy fast.

■■■

Chapter 2

Big War Games, Little War Games, and What Did They Do Without Computers[1]?

The U.S. military's Millennium Challenge '02, conducted over three weeks in 2002, was the largest and most complex war game simulation ever carried out by a military. With 13,500 participants and a price tag of $250 million, the exercise was aimed at testing the various U.S. services' abilities to collaborate in war fighting tactics against an unnamed Middle East opponent.

Talk about a large-scale war game: The Millennium Challenge involved nine live-force "battles" conducted at military training bases against U.S. soldiers standing in as the enemy.

It goes without saying that the opponent (the Red Team), was meant to lose. Military leadership under then–Secretary of Defense, Donald Rumsfeld, was using the game to prepare for a transformation of the U.S. military into a 21st-century technological powerhouse, and they did not expect to be handed a loss by a Middle Eastern army. The Americans held an overwhelming advantage in force size, strength, and sophistication.

But, as the American Revolution proved, better uniforms don't win wars, and you don't need computers and high-powered consultants to lose a war. Mere blind spots will do.

The ragtag *imaginary* Red Team forces were led by Paul Van Riper, who retired from the Marines in 1997 after serving as head of the Corps' Combat Development Command. Van Riper recognized all of the advantages possessed by

American forces. He also knew that the home team's reliance on technology left it exposed to deceptively simple tactics. When the Blue Team's naval force (the good guys) sailed into the Persian Gulf early in the game, Van Riper surrounded the fleet with small boats and planes, floating and flying innocently around the warships. The Blue commander issued an ultimatum to surrender. Van Riper called for an attack via the morning call to prayer, and those small boats and planes turned on the fleet, overwhelming the Blues with kamikaze attacks.

With the Blue naval forces now sitting on the ocean floor, Van Riper commenced to wage the kind of war that the United States has been fighting for several years later in Iraq: an unsettling, low-tech insurgency that blurs the lines between civilian and military forces. Red forces were constantly on the move, defying Blue's attempts to set up coherent battles. To evade U.S. eavesdropping technology, Van Riper used messengers to convey information across the theater of battle: The bad guys rode motorcycles and did not use military communication gear.

Van Riper's strategy provoked military planners to intervene more actively in the game—re-floating the Blue navy after the suicide attacks, for instance, and forcing Van Riper to turn off his air-defense systems at one point to permit a Blue attack. The Red and Blue teams were ordered to follow a *script*. Instead of running a realistic war game, as they should have, the Pentagon decided to run a *rehearsal*.Van Riper resigned soon after, and the game was deemed a success by Rumsfeld and his consultants. The United States has paid an enormous price in the years following, as the war in Iraq proved how unprepared it was for the insurgency in Iraq.

In retrospect, taxpayers would probably have found better use for $250,000,000. Maybe buy a small-scale war game with no computer simulations but with *real* role-playing? Some defense experts scoff at a notion of what they call "bunch of guys sitting around a table" type war games. So one must wonder: What did planners do before they had all that wonderful technology and mobility? After all, war games are an ancient art. What did they do in the pre-computer/big consultants' days? How did Field Marshall Montgomery win in North Africa against superior forces in World War II with only a sand table and a bunch of guys standing around it, without all those sophisticated algorithms and defense contractors? Okay, they were British, true, but still….

Must be a mystery for a "bunch of guys *running* around," spending a quarter of a billion dollars.

Famous Military War Games

The art of war gaming is an old art. Artifacts from the Sumerian civilization suggest that military leaders have been scratching out simulated battles for many thousands of years. War games played an important role in Prussia's rise to military power during the 18th century. Frederick the Great of Prussia actually took a mobile war gaming toolkit with him to all of his military operations. This toolkit was a box with "tactical war game" (*taktisches Kriegsspiel*) written on it. It contained model armies, landscapes, and other miniature features of a battlefield. This box can still be viewed in one of Frederick's palaces. Frederick the Great was feared for his hard-to-predict but accurate battle field moves. Prussia won some decisive victories over numerically and economically superior rivals, especially Austria. In the decades after Frederick the Great passed away, his sons still used war games to prepare battles, but then the art slowly declined in Prussia. Legend has it that, when Napoleon Bonaparte conquered Prussia in the early 19th century, he visited Frederick's grave and stated. "If you were alive, I would not be standing here."[2] He probably knew what he was talking about.

So did the Prussians, as war gaming reemerged in the late 19th century and played an important role in the Franco-Prussian

War of 1870–71. Using war games to prepare their operations, the Prussian army crafted superior maneuvers, innovative methods of transportation, and even improved procedures for disease control among its troops, all of which led to a crushing defeat for the French army. But the most important impact of Prussia's strategic excellence was felt in the political preparation of the Franco-Prussian War. Otto von Bismarck, the "Iron Chancellor" of Prussia, was famous as well as notorious for his insistence on basing every political, diplomatic, and military move on a profound understanding of underlying dynamics and *likely responses*. He would have been shocked to find out how some large corporations and smart executives use made-up assumptions about their opponents or made-up mathematical equilibrium solutions to fight their market "battles." Under Bismarck's lead, Prussia was able to politically isolate France and other rivals, making them an easier target. Bismarck went down in the history books as one of the few strategists to have reached his war's goals. He united Germany into a single nation-state.

Little Wars

War gaming was never confined to large wars and big nations. Similar to war games at the product level, which are advocated in this manual, the Israeli hostage rescue operation in Entebbe, Uganda, shows just how the art *should* be practiced.

On June 27, 1976, Air France Flight 139 from Tel Aviv to Paris was hijacked by a mixed crew of German and Palestinian terrorists who boarded the plane during a stopover at Athens. After a short stop in Libya, the hijacked plane landed in Entebbe, Uganda, where the hijackers enjoyed the hospitality of Idi Amin, the country's notorious dictator (role-played, brilliantly, years later by Oscar winner Forest Whitaker. He should have been running the Millennium Challenge game.).

The hostages were taken off the plane and into the airport's old terminal building, which was guarded by Ugandan soldiers. The terrorists demanded the release of convicted comrades throughout the world. The Israeli government could not fulfill these demands even if it wanted to (and it definitely did not want to). The hijackers released the non-Jewish passengers, and threatened to execute the Jewish passengers if their demands were not met by July 4th.

Israeli commandos had but a few days to make plans for a complicated rescue mission in a place thousands of miles away, on a different continent. The planners quickly built a replica of the Entebbe terminal; they involved an Israeli general who knew Idi Amin personally and debriefed Israeli businesspeople who visited Uganda. They were lucky: They did not have $250 million and they never met the Pentagon's habitual defense *experts*. They did not even use computers.

Instead, the Israeli military planners role-played the situation from all perspectives: from a low-ranking Ugandan sentry to a high-ranking Ugandan officer. They assessed the hijackers' state of mind based on intelligence extracted from impromptu interviews with the released non-Jewish hostages in Europe. The operation was scheduled to be a late-night operation, in part because the war game concluded, from role-playing the Ugandans, that Ugandan radar operators would look for a reason to *not* wake up General Amin (to avoid his wrath in the event of a false alarm). After all, no one believed Israeli soldiers would be crazy enough to fly into Uganda.

The night before the terrorists' ultimatum ran out, the Israeli Defense Forces (IDF) launched their trip to Africa. Timing was critical: The lead aircraft would touch down between one commercial aircraft's take off and another one's landing. It was highly unlikely that the Ugandans would switch off the runway lights between these two events. The illuminated runway made things easier. The first commando aircraft carried a black Mercedes and a few Land Rovers, resembling Idi Amin's presidential convoy. Their engines were started while the plane was still in the air. The commando force did not want to lose time on the ground for engine trouble, especially with the Mercedes limousine; that car was "borrowed" from a civilian only two days earlier. Immediately following the first plane touchdown, while it was still moving, the "president and his escorts" drove out toward the old terminal where the hostages were held. The commando force raided the terminal like a lightning strike. They killed all terrorists as well as Ugandan soldiers who turned their weapons against them. The terminal was taken first, with more parts of the airport following in short succession.

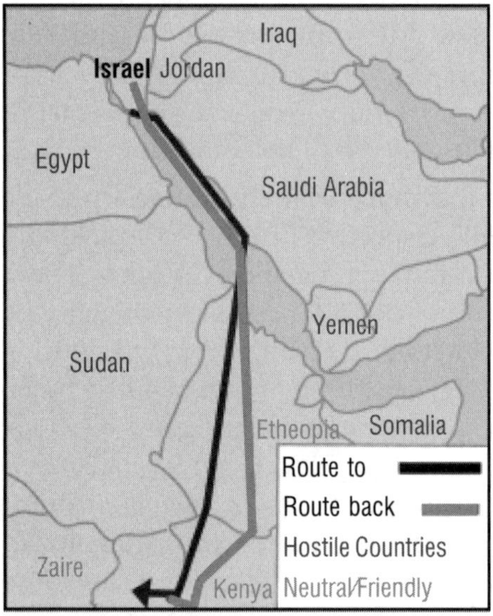

The Israeli commando raid's route.

The Ugandan airfield troops, after recovering from the initial shock, decided to turn off the runway lights to stop the Israelis from landing additional aircrafts with reinforcements. One can only imagine their surprise when it turned out the first commandos had placed battery-powered lights next to the runway lights. The lights stayed on.

The airfield security forces were quickly overwhelmed. The next *likely* reaction for the Ugandan military—war gamed in advance by the Israelis—would have been to try to regain control of the airport. As the whole operation took not much longer than one and a half hours on the ground, only a very quick intervention of local forces would have been a threat to the Israeli rescue mission. Such a fast reaction could be undertaken by Ugandan units stationed near the Entebbe airport, on the road to Kampala, the country's capital. The Israeli soldiers ambushed the road leading to the Ugandan military base. The Ugandans could forget about reinforcing their airfield forces.

To counter one last threat to the operation, the Israeli commandos "convinced" Ugandan air force pilots to take the rest of the day off by blowing up all fighter planes stationed in Entebbe. This was to prevent any attempt to pursue the Israelis on their way home.

The Israelis took off, stopping for a refuel in nearby Kenya. There, the IDF medical corps already waited with a Boeing aircraft converted into a flying hospital, ready to treat any wounded. All contingencies were worked out during the war game. Nothing was left to chance.

As the Israelis showed the world, the true art of war gaming is to find a strategic path to success that is neither optimistic nor pessimistic but *realistic*. It's based on realistic reading of opponents' mind set, motivation, limitations, and *likely* actions. Corporate, take heed!

Tiny War Games

Back in the early 20th century, H.G. Wells published two books, *Floor Games* (1911) and *Little Wars* (1913), that offered a set of rules for playing war games using toy soldiers.

Wells wrote *Little Wars* wearily, a genius ahead of his time. He reported that important battles were sometimes interrupted "by a great rustle and chattering of lady visitors. They regarded the objects upon the floor with the empty disdain of their sex for all imaginative things."[3] One cannot really blame those ladies. The spectacle of two middle-aged men playing with "toy soldiers" on the floor, and very heated and excited about it, as Wells confessed, was probably quite unsettling.

Wells damned the military simulations of the British Army, in a way that would resonate with critics of the Pentagon and its "experts" or corporate executives and their big budget war games:

They tell me—what I already a little suspected—that Kriegspiel, as it is played by the British Army, is a very dull and unsatisfactory exercise, lacking in realism, in stir and the unexpected, obsessed by the umpire at every turn, and of very doubtful value in waking up the imagination, which should be its chief function.[4]

Indeed, put Wells in a typical game theory or Monte Carlo Simulated environment and he would have laughed his head off. Or maybe cried. Strategy, it was clear to Wells, was about imagination, not following a script or feeding generic moves to a hypothetical market model!

War Games in a Different Context

We have covered various angles of what war games have meant to mankind—in military history, diplomacy, and even leisure activities—but the introduction would not be complete without a look over the fence to see if such techniques of planning and strategic thinking have a meaning for other species as well. Animals war gaming, you ask? Well, yes.

Great white sharks hunt sea lions. They show an ability to at least act in patterns that resemble those of a war gaming strategist: *thinking ahead of the potential response from the other player*. Great whites often wait for sea lions to try to swim out to sea, and away from the bay where they have carved themselves a piece of rock territory for mating and giving birth. No sea lion can go to another's rock without encountering fierce resistance, as sea lions are very territorial.

A great white shark always seems to match a sea lion to its rock. The shark only injures the sea lion in its initial attack. Though the shark is much stronger than the sea lion, the latter can still cause injury in an outright fight to the death. The shark has no interest in a tough fight. Instead, he lets go of the sea lion and waits for him, close to the sea lion's home rock. His prey wants to get out of the water. But when the sea lion approaches what looks to be safety—worn down by panic and injury from the first attack—the waiting shark finishes off what it began earlier in the open sea. The only sea lions surviving such a maneuver are those that swim out to sea to recover, instead of trying to reach their "safe" rock. On these rare occasions the shark is waiting in the wrong place. This indicates that the shark does not simply follow his prey, but engages in a strategy of responding to the *most likely* move by the sea lion.

Now the question: Is your company the shark or is it the sea lion?

The Move to Business War Games

As Wells observed, small-scale battles can be deeply satisfying for the gladiators involved and, done properly, they can even improve the outcomes of actual wars. General George S. Patton's ascent to glory started in the area of East Texas–West Louisiana where General McNair played his war game in 1942. Through a series of brilliant moves played in this war game, Patton developed his famous maneuvers, which heavily influenced the war in Europe. Yet for many years following Wells's books the thrill of small-scale victory was largely absent from *corporate boardrooms*. Why was that so?

We humbly suggest pointing fingers at our colleagues in finance.

The discipline of finance has led the charge in responding to the post–World War II world of business, on two fronts: mitigating risk (corporate finance), and influencing the top executive discourse.

The risk piece, despite fits and starts, has generally worked well during the past 30 years:

- New financial instruments have given companies a new way to manage risk and expand their reach. Puts and calls, hedging of inputs (think Southwest and the price of oil), weather futures, and, of course, the use of options.
- Financial modeling and credit scoring allowed better risk management for lenders. Bank-based credit card lenders, for example, took a bath in earlier recessions, but made a bunch of money in the 1990s.
- The creative use of capital markets allowed companies to spread risk. The Capital Asset Pricing Model is the big example. A more-specific example is how mortgage-backed securities solved the problem of spreading out the payment streams during the life of the bonds.

This quantitative-based success has been impressive enough to persuade many companies that risk is a financial issue. CFOs became chief risk officers by default.

But the influence of finance did not stop at risk management. Top executives, ever more comfortable with financial discussion and financial manipulation through stock buyouts and M&A activities, have turned to financial-based discussion at the core of their strategy-making. With that, top executives have all but abandoned looking at the world. If it is not in the numbers (crunched daily), it does not exist. It does not matter. The most balanced companies in the world have been failing left and right, watching their own numbers flickering on the executive screens.

There are important and legitimate issues of planning that must be resolved by the financial function. For instance, even a basic forecast of customer demand can make a huge difference in capital investment decisions. Likewise, the cost structure of a business can change significantly based on expectations of future prices of inputs. Look no further than fuel prices in the airline industry as a painful example. We really *do* want the gang with the green lampshades to cultivate a view of the world as it may look in the near future. But reducing strategy to a series of discounted cash flows (DCF), real options (the new game in town), or good old estimated profit-and-loss statements is a recipe for disaster. Just look at Enron, a wizard of P&Ls and forward-looking financial planning.

While finance was marching on, and newly minted MBAs coming to dominate all discussions on the strategic level, the strategic planning piece has not worked as well. From its origin with GE in the 1960s, strategic planning has not advanced much. Some may say, quite accurately, it actually retreated.

Do not misunderstand. I love accounting and finance. Some of my closest friends are accountants. They are lovely people. On their watch, however, strategic planning has gone to the dogs. Instead, companies were pushed to execute, to act, to move fast, without much thinking, but with hallucinatory *spreadsheets. Thinking* has degraded to the point that businesspeople have to be reminded of its virtues from time to time. Efficiency expert Julie Morgenstern laments the information overload environment in companies today: "This new environment doesn't encourage stepping back and being strategic.... People respond to the thing that's screaming the loudest. It's reactive. And being reactive isn't smart."[5] Her advice: "Fight for your right to think."[6]

The first return to thinking should be in the form of a real, hard-knocks business war game, a real outthinking the competition in the real world. It can be done superbly with a bunch of guys sitting around a table if they use the REALIST criterion from Chapter 1. This book offers you the "how," but you need to fill in the "what." Do not surrender the "what" to imaginary modeling, computer algorithms, an army of MBAs in expensive suits, or complacency in the form of naval gazing: "We know what's going on; we've been in this market for years."

Part II

Competitors as Characters

Chapter 3

Can You Accurately Predict Competitors' Moves?

Would I write this book if you could not predict competitors' moves? The answer to the chapter title is yes—you definitely can.

In a recent article in one of the popular business presses, an executive gushed about a prediction made during one of those large-scale computer-assisted games for senior management. The model apparently predicted an acquisition of some assets by a competitor. I got a good chuckle out of that executive's amazement. That type of prediction is literally child's play. If you stick to a rigorous analytical frame, specific intelligence about the character of the competition, and a few simple rules of role-playing, you can make much more difficult predictions. The theory leads you to make the predictions with the highest probability of occurring.

Can you predict 100 percent of competitors' moves? No. The reason is not only that, to get to that level, you need inside information, which is illegal. The reason is much more prosaic: Think of your own company. Can you predict your own executives' decisions with 100-percent accuracy?

But the question is actually irrelevant. You don't need 100-percent accuracy to improve your plan's odds of success. All you need is a realistic and pragmatic assessment of competitors' most likely responses.

Start Here

Competitors' moves do not happen in a vacuum. They happen within the context of your industry, or market. One of the striking differences between computerized or theoretical war games and your real war games is the perspective you take on the market. So in every war game, ask the teams to quickly analyze the market's underlying trends, as outlined here, before they delve into competitors' specific moves. You'd be surprised how well market analysis allows you to frame competitors' actions, and how important this is for your own plan.

Market Imbalance

Theories of market behavior can be roughly divided into two types: neoclassical equilibrium theories (including variants such as game theory and decisions under uncertainty) and Schumpeterian market theories (named for Joseph A. Schempeter, author of *Capitalism, Socialism and Democracy* [Harper & Row, 1942]). Traditional (neoclassical) theories imagine the market at or moving towards equilibrium, where a "stable" balance among the major players (buyers and suppliers, demand and supply) is achieved. In a stable market, opportunities are exhausted and rates of return tend to equalize, and *there is no intrinsic reason to change the situation.* The Schumpeterian theory, on the other hand, regards markets as in a *constant* state of flux, where the balance of power among the various parties is always shifting through the discovery of disequilibrium opportunities, what Schumpeter called "creative destruction."

The process of discovering market opportunities is the entrepreneurial process, aptly described by Israel Kirzner as a process by which information and expectations are continually changing, and error, ignorance, and/or luck allows alert individuals (or their companies) to take advantage of market imbalances. Without error or ignorance on the part of *some* market participants, and without information being available differently to different individuals, a quest for profitable strategy is futile. Think about the record industry. While the record companies believed the market was stable, or in "equilibrium," buyers of music were discontent. They wanted to buy single tracks of preferred music and not a whole package of 12 songs on a CD. When the Internet-based music "reaping" of single songs became available, buyers flocked to online services (legal or not). Only in retrospect did suppliers of music realize the disequilibrium pressure, which existed all along. The ignorance or error of the large music companies enabled the profits of such companies as iTunes and Rhapsody and the whole Internet file-sharing phenomenon.

Competitors' moves take place against their assumptions and expectations regarding the market disequilibrium opportunities. Your plan should be based on your assumptions and expectations of the disequilibrium opportunities (and risks). At the end of the day, the one that is less blind wins. In analyzing competitors, try to see *their* perspective on where the market is going.

What Causes Markets' Constant Imbalance?

In order to investigate market imbalances and how they affect competitors' strategic positioning, one has to adopt a model of an underlying market structure. Though it is not the only market model, Michael Porter's Five Forces model of industry analysis is a good starting point. In this model, Porter posits that the attractiveness of industries depend on the pressures exerted by five forces: buyers (and end-users if different), suppliers, new entrants, substitute industries, and the intensity of industry's rivalry. Companies neutralize the pressures or lose profitability as buyers push for lower prices, suppliers push for higher prices, new entrants try to grab market share, and substitutes attempt to persuade customers to switch to their products. The intensity of rivalry ebbs and flows as players formulate strategies to position themselves optimally against the four external forces and their evolution through time.

Adopting the Schumpeterian market theory, we assume that the balance of power among the five forces is at best precarious and most likely misleading; it *hides* disequilibrium risks and opportunities. In other words, at any moment in time forces are at work changing this balance. What you see is *not* what you get. Various moves of the players in the industry in anticipation of (real or imaginary) external transformation of technology, government regulations, and social and demographic characteristics are continually driving change in any market's balance of power. If the players themselves do not initiate change, new entrants may capitalize on their blind spots. Google's strategy of simplifying search technology capitalized on Yahoo's conviction that customers will always want human editorial help rather than searching the Web themselves. While Yahoo focused on creating categories of "content," Google sneaked in and took away the audience.

Though the balance of power in all industries is continually shifting, it is not easy to discern. The gap between customers' needs and available supply may be growing, but its signals are often weak, confusing, ambiguous, and hard to interpret. If they weren't, everyone would grab them instantly, and the hypothetical world of neoclassical equilibrium would become real. During a war game, teams should try to identify as many weak signals as possible. Predicting competitors' moves and countermoves is more productive if done in the context of their expectations of where the market is going. It prevents the common tendency to predict that competitors will simply continue with their current strategies.

So you should ask questions such as these: What is changing in the market? Which forces are growing in strength (and importance)? Which competitors seem to position themselves to capitalize on the opportunities brought about by the shifting balance? Which competitors seem oblivious to those shifts?

This last question is especially important because it can be turned inward: Do we agree on these shifts? Are we prepared for them? Is my plan robust enough to survive those shifts? *Does it take advantage of them?* For example, in every war game I ran in the consumer and food industry, participants identified the consolidation and rising power of the large retail chains as a major disequilibrium trend, pushing the industry out of balance. While everyone agreed (or lamented) about this sorry state, few stopped to think: "Can we take advantage of it? Is my plan addressing this issue?" Myopic launches of new products without explicit attention to this disequilibrium shift are, well, myopic. When the honeymoon phase following the introduction and flurry of promotions is over, how do you keep the retailer interested? Some creative and practical ideas regarding the harnessing the power of the retailers came out of games where the retailer's perspective was explicitly addressed. For example, one can actually *capitalize*—and some market players such as P&G actually do—on clubs' and discount chains' desire to severely reduce the number of brands carried in each store.

Once you have charted the industry's landscape and participants agreed on the salient disequilibrium trends, you can move the focus to specific competitors: How are they positioned in the current industry structure? What they are *likely to do* in light of the upcoming "tectonic shifts" in the market? The frameworks that follow should help in answering these questions.

The Most Predictive Theory of Competitors' Behavior

Through the years, management gurus and academics proposed various frameworks to predicting competitor's strategies, from McKinsey 7s, to BCG growth-share matrix, to GE's variation on those, but none has come even close to the predictive power of Michael Porter's pioneering Four Corners Model.

The full exposition of Porter's model can be found in his seminal book, *Competitive Strategy* (Free Press, 1980). In recent years, a growing body of research on human cognitive processes has added strong support to Porter's modeling. This combination of psychology, neuroscience, and strategic modeling gives you powerful tools in the quest to predict competitors' moves and responses.

Porter's model posits that competitors' behavior is influenced by 4 antecedents or "corners" in a balance-sheet type table, such as this one:

The Antecedents of Competitors' Behavior

Motivation	Observed behavior
• Drivers • Management assumptions	• Current strategy • Capabilities

On the right-hand side, competitors' observed behavior in the market (such as its current strategy and its capabilities) predicts a lot of its future behavior. A significant part of future strategy is a continuation of current strategy, as most companies run on inertia, and modification to strategy is almost always tactical and incremental, at "the margin." Current capabilities give a good starting point to predict what a competitor will regard as "core capabilities" and how future buildup of capabilities will look. Capabilities include both operational (manufacturing, customer service, technology/R&D, marketing, and so on by functional area) and financial (financial ratios, cost of capital, cash flow, and so forth). Capabilities also expose commitments, such as investment in particular technologies, assets, and agreements with third parties, and these are important in understanding *constraints and limitations* (more on that later).

If you are less than impressed, that's understandable. Using current strategy and capabilities to predict future strategy and capabilities is the common practice in almost every firm. It's the most intuitive type of prediction. In earlier days of war gaming, I would go around the company interviewing executives about what they regarded as competitors' goals and intentions. The input they provided evolved almost exclusively around those obvious increments around existing strategies and capabilities, and the predictions accordingly were often poor. The reason was that, in reacting to a company's move, competitors often acted out of motives and assumptions that were not quite "rational" in the sense of a cost-benefit analysis with full information and a "preference optimizing" equilibrium solution (this is economists' lingo). Despite being an economist by training, Porter realized deliberate, rational decision-making was often the tip of an iceberg. He strongly advocated a behavioral economics approach to predicting economic behavior. Behavioral economics is a branch of economics that adds social sciences to the investigation of economic behavior.

Porter called for understanding what *motivates* the competition (see the left-hand side in the previous table) by examining drivers of corporate behavior and the mind set of company's decision makers (aka "management assumptions"). In his analysis, he included goals, internal culture and value system, executives' background, organizational dynamics, historical roots and commitments, board members' profiles, identity of the consulting firms habitually influencing executive thinking, and attitude toward risks, as well as management beliefs about the industry and its own position in it. In the broadest sense, Porter advocated a closer look at what neuroscientists term automatic or unobserved processes, underlying observed behavior.

New Neuroscience Research

In the past decade, brain neurological research made big strides in advancing our understanding of decision process. The way human beings behave reflects the outcome of two (at times competing) brain activities: cognition and affect. Cognitive activity involves reasoning. Affective activity involves "passions": emotions and feelings (fear, anger, love) and biological drives (sex, hunger, pain). Both cognitive and affective processes come in two forms: deliberate and automatic. Deliberate processes are controlled by the consciousness. They are serial, require effort, and are relatively slow (for example, a financial cost-benefit calculation). Automatic processes are parallel, effortless, rapid, and *not accessible to conscious reflection* (for example, an intuitive liking of a certain person or idea). The result is the following four brain activities:

- Automatic cognitive.
- Deliberate cognitive.
- Automatic affective.
- Deliberate affective.

Deliberate cognitive activities control rational thinking, such as calculations of economic value added (EVA) of projects. Deliberate affective activities intervene mostly when one tries, for example, to deliberately imagine past emotional experiences in order to understand another person's feelings (such as in *method* acting). The automatic cognitive process is a reflexive processing of percepts, such as in visual identification, language understanding, or quick physical reactions. Automatic affective activities apply where affects (feelings and moods) automatically create impressions based on memory and drives' states. Each processing can be traced roughly to different areas in the brain. Behavior results from the interaction of the four activities, interaction that includes collaboration and at time competition for the scarce resource of attention. Automatic processes are always active, underneath our consciousness. Higher order controlled processes may, or may not, intervene to correct or override automatic processes. The following example can serve as a rough approximation to this overall process.

You are sitting in a conference room, and a colleague presents an overview of a new market into which your company is considering an entry. The boss is in the room as well. As the first slide goes up on the screen, your auto cognition quickly and automatically figures out what is presented. The visual signals are decoded and compared with stored images that allow you to recognize the shape of a growth curve in this market. Auto affect then brings affect to bear on the image, so that your brain automatically attaches "reward value" to what you identified as a growth curve. Your personal history with growth projections and the presenter in the past will have an input. Your current level of fear of failure will have an input. Even your physical state (biological drives' state) will affect your perception (anger, for example, makes people less risk-adverse; sadness makes them more). Processing may end at this point, as processing often ends before controlled activities intervene, and you may express strong enthusiasm for the idea presented by the colleague. However, if you have seen a recent memo on the regulatory climate or quality problems in this new market, you may express a more cautionary view (deliberate cognitive activity). Or, if you have seen such a memo but consider the colleague a close ally, you may support his idea temporarily, despite your reservation, expecting his disappointment if you said something bad in front of the boss (deliberate affective activity).

The new research adds two important dimensions to Porter's Four Corners model. First, it is clear that, when making predictions about a company's moves, one needs to take into account *implicit* factors, corresponding to human automatic processes (both cognitive and affective). Just as observed human behavior cannot be explained or predicted based on deliberate, controlled reasoning alone, companies' behavior cannot be explained by rational financial reasoning alone. Porter understood that well: His revolutionary insistence on accounting for culture, history, executive, consultants, and board's backgrounds, goals, values and commitments, and his inclusion of management deep beliefs and assumptions about what works or does not work in the market, are clearly in line with the effect of underlying "automatic" or *implicit* factors on companies' future behavior. Alas, despite Porter's apparent popularity, the vast majority of executives and analysts stick to the easy-to-get *observed* behavior as the sole basis to thinking about competition. The disproportionate emphasis put on financial intelligence, for example (competitors' P&L and balance sheets), reveals a methodical lack of understanding of what truly predicts competitors' moves. In war games, those managers who rely heavily on financial or econometric modeling to predict corporate moves tend to be the poorest forecasters.

The second contribution of the new research to Porter's model is more subtle, and depends on your belief regarding decision-making in corporations. A company is a collective of many individuals, but it behaves according to the whims and vagaries of just a few decision-makers: the CEO (in the case of a corporation), the division or SBU's president (in the case of business units), and possibly one or two additional "inner circle" executives or advisors (such as a trusted investment banker or senior partner in a consulting firm). The decisions of these powerful individuals at the end are subject to the influences of affective and automatic processes described by neuroscientists. Recall the quote in Chapter 1 from Bossidy and Charan, two experienced business leaders, about the high prevalence of powerful decision-makers who misread reality and doom good research and careful decision processes. These executives are human and, despite the temptation to view corporate decisions as rational and economic-based, the truth is these decisions reflect a lot more personal effect. Angry executives take more risks, emotional executives make rush judgments, and biased executives use rationalization to explain decisions that were actually driven by automatic processes in their cortex, such as their past history, their physical drives, a quick pattern matching, or attention biases to which they have *no introspective access*. Can you otherwise explain Gerald Levine's decision to sell Time-Warner to AOL for peanuts? Jean Paul Messier of Vivendi's out-of-control empire building, which brought the proud company to its knees? Juergen Schrempp's, the powerful chairman and CEO of Daimler, decision to buy Chrysler for a price that proved 100 percent too much?

Not convinced? Here is one of the best examples of a decision made without the decision-makers having introspective access to their own true (and biased) processing. A 2003 study of gifts given to physicians by pharmaceutical companies reveals amazing results.[1] Physicians in this study adamantly denied being influenced in their prescription practices by those gifts despite *experimental evidence to the contrary*. The authors then posed a simple and powerful question that you should reflect on if your tendency is to believe managerial decisions are solely rational and fully cognitively accessible: Would pharmaceutical companies continue to throw hundreds of millions of dollars year after year on those gifts if *they did not work*? If you answered yes, you just confirmed the irrational behavior of companies. If you answered no, the physicians have rationalized behavior that was actually different than what they perceived.

The neuroscientists are quite clear on one thing: "The struggle between rapid unconscious pattern-detection processes and their slow, effortful modulation by deliberation is not a fair contest; so automatic impressions will influence behavior much of the time."[2] Executives (and their communication departments) may have a strong need to *rationalize* their decisions, but that does not mean they acted out of rational consideration. As one competitive intelligence manager in a large energy company put it: Give the executives spreadsheets and they can make a case for anything according to their prior beliefs. So, in analyzing competitors, pay close attention to the left-hand side of Porter's Four Corners Model if you want to make accurate predictions. In the next chapters, we will elaborate on what information can help you sketch competitors' implicit influences.

Do You Need Role-Playing?

With this combination of analytics and neuroscience at your disposal, do you really need to role-play competitors? Wouldn't it be just a straightforward task of analysis? Besides, role-playing does not sound too...serious.

The fact is, it is serious business, because predicting competitors' moves requires an extra ingredient:

Predicting competitors' actions requires the ability to "read" others' minds, and, apparently, we are not all born equal with regard to this ability.

This is the most striking finding from recent research in neuroscience: There is a special ability called "mentalizing" that allows people to infer what other people will feel or do. The fact that the brain has a specialized process for mentalizing others (called Theory of Mind) was discovered during studies of autistic children. In one interesting experiment, the researchers showed pairs of children an object and then let them see where it was concealed. One of the pair is then asked to leave the room, and, while he or she is outside, the researcher moves the object to a new location, in full view of the remaining child. The remaining child is then asked to predict where the child coming back to the room will look for the object. In other words, the child is asked to predict the behavior of another person. Non-autistic children make correct predictions at ages

3 to 4. Autistic children are able to make such predictions much later (ages 8 to 12) and with great difficulty. More intriguing, autistic children can easily predict that a photo taken of the object before it was moved would show the object in its old location, not the new one. So it is reading the *other's* mind that is lacking. Studies with patients with lesions in a specific brain area further hint that mentalizing has its own separate module in the brain, located in what is known as Brodmann 10 area in the frontal cortex.[3]

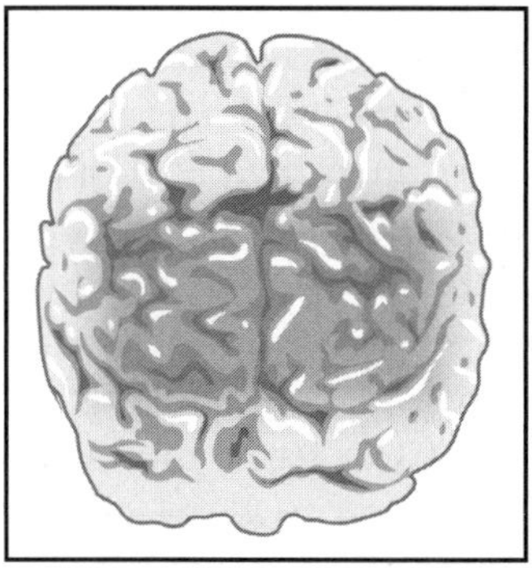

Broadmann 10 area

Mirror Imaging

If the ability to "read minds" is differential in people, it means that a mere logical-deductive reasoning about other people's actions based on one's preferences may be too simplistic. In other words, mirror thinking ("if we were in their shoes that is what we would do *because it makes the most sense to us*") is not good enough in the competitive race to predict competitors' (and customers', and regulators', and partners') actions. The implications to most computer-based war games that require input from executives regarding competitors' intentions are quite damaging. The "Theory of the Mind" talent, which some people exhibit naturally more than others, suggests that intuitive, superficial convictions and beliefs about competitors are largely useless. See if you can relate to the difference in the following two statements:

- "If we were in their shoes that is what we would do *because it makes the most sense to us*."
- "If we were in their shoes that is what we would do *because it would have made the most sense to them*."

To most practical managers, the difference may seem semantic or even trivial. To a seasoned intelligence officer, the difference is real. This is why war gaming participants may find an unlikely area—techniques borrowed from great acting teachers—interesting. Though these techniques may not replace an innate talent of putting oneself into another's mindset, they may help those without the talent to make better predictions. I will distill some of these ideas in the next chapter. For those who are turned off by this business of "acting," rest assured we are not talking about elaborate acting lessons or making a war game into a Broadway play. Far from it. But I do want you to think about the following, before you dismiss "acting like a competitor" as a gimmick: Actors can spend months and sometime *years* preparing to role play one character in a movie, so that their characterization is as close as possible to reality. Companies spend 20 minutes reassuring themselves that they know what competitors will do. And yet acting is not serious?

Managerial Biases

Why bother with analytical frameworks at all? Seasoned managers who've been in the market many years consider themselves experts, and rightfully so. However, in the past two decades, a large body of research in decision theory and behavioral economics has confirmed consistent biases in judgments made by individuals, including managers. This body of knowledge, pioneered with the research of two Israeli Nobel Prize laureates, Daniel Kahneman and Amos Tversky, has significant implications to our war gaming.

Every manager who has ever put together a plan, or was part of a team putting together a plan that had to survive competitive pressures had made assumptions about how competitors will react, what their moves were going to be (regardless of their specific reaction to the plan), and how other players (customers, consumers, regulators, and so on) were going to act in the time horizon covered by the plan. Unless one is totally into naval gazing, no manager plans without regard to competitors or other parties' reactions. The problem is that, without a rigorous framework to guide this thinking, research shows that managers are likely to fall into the following traps:

1. *Intuition takes over.* Intuition means that more easily accessible images, thoughts, and beliefs about competitors and customers will dominate the managers' thinking. Research suggests that people are not accustomed to thinking hard, and are "often content to trust a plausible judgment that quickly comes to mind."[4] Many of those "plausible" judgments turn out to be dead wrong. If you want intuition, skip the war game. Just call a few people and ask for their opinions, and then do what you decided to do anyway. It is called the Delphi method in professional forecasters' circles.

2. *Emotions take over.* The subject of competition is an emotional one for most managers (the Godfather's claim of "it is business, not personal" notwithstanding). Emotions create "motivated cognitions"; people convince themselves that "what they would like to happen is what will happen."[5] In the competition between affect and thinking, affect wins hands down. As one researcher summed it up: "Where thought conflicts with emotion, the latter is designed by the neural circuitry in our brain to win."[6]

3. *Over-optimism takes over.* Because people lack introspection into automatic processes that produce cognitive biases in their judgment (such as strong emotions or first impressions), they are good at self-deception and self-manipulation.[7] There is evidence that some people, especially senior executives, have their attention—which is largely controlled by automatic processes in the brain—drawn to information that is favorable to them. The results are

chronic over-optimistic predictions. Sometimes optimism is a great asset; some other times it is not. The problem is those optimistic executives can't tell the difference.

4. *Myopia takes over.* Strategic thinking requires iterations: You do one thing, the opponent does another, you respond, it responds, and so on. Strategic iterations require memory, which is a scarce resource, and the ability to put oneself in the other side's place, which we've already seen is a special skill. Experimental evidence suggests that a "default" of only one to two steps of strategic thinking is typical.[8] Market battles typically involve more than one or two moves and countermoves. There is evidence that training (such as provided by a theoretical framework) increases the number of iterations people are capable of conceiving to three or four. However, most managers are not trained and therefore war games that go beyond two to three steps become science fiction, not science.

So use a state-of-the-art theory of competitors' real behavior, or save your money and read tea leaves. If you then boil them, you also have a healthy drink.

The Secret to Amazing Predictions

Okay. You've crossed the analytical bridge, running a competitor through Porter's Four Corners Model, paying close attention to the implicit influences on the competitor's management thinking. The intelligence provided by your intelligence professionals was sufficient to allow for exercising role-playing techniques, which advanced your ability to predict the character's moves up several notches. What do you do with all this information?

The answer is, of course, you predict competitor's moves. But how do you move from understanding the character of the competition to predictions? The art here is that of *narrowing down* the possibilities to those *most likely* moves. That's an important advantage of realistic games over hypothetical or theoretical ones.

In the space of all possible moves by a competitor, some moves will be more likely then others. Some moves will have zero (or almost zero) probability of occurring. And some moves will be certain (close to 100-percent probability). Remember the following rule of thumb:

Predicting competitors' moves is similar to predicting hurricanes.

In predicting a hurricane path, the meteorological service uses different colors to denote changing level of certainty. The red zone is certain hit, and the orange zone is between 50- and 99-percent probabilities. This is where your war game predictions are aimed, because these are the areas requiring *action*. Whereas hypothetical mathematical models look at all ranges of potential actions, or generate random events as "surprises," war games look at real likely ones where you need to modify your plan to meet most likely challenges to it. The next section is an example of the layers of analysis using our methodologies.

So, What Are Competitors Most Likely to Do?

Answering the following three questions focuses the war game on competitors' most likely responses, and significantly increases the predictive power of a game.

Question # 1: "Is the Competitor Satisfied With its Present Position in the Market?"

Porter's theory suggests that management that assumes its strategy is working and its market position is healthy will be less likely to redraw strategy in a radical way. It is common sense. It is easier to predict complacent management's future actions than it is a company in various states of reorganizing, restructuring, and *re-leadershipping*. However, judging management's state of mind regarding its market position is not easy. One should note *not* to rely too heavily on annual reports as a source of intelligence for answering this question. Think of annual reports as you would the glossy covers of fashion magazines: The models and actresses are retouched to the point of fiction. Annual reports, numerical content aside for a moment, are basically propaganda for the masses—in this case the investing masses. I regard them as useful only in sequence: Comparing the "letter from the CEO" over several years may be revealing as to which issues are transitory and which are strategic.

First-timers to the art of intelligence tend to answer Question 1 in the negative, based on the fact that most CEOs express a need to improve, to increase, to change, to face challenges, etc., etc, etc. Yet experience suggests that most CEOs improve or increase or change little. (Cost-cutting does not count as a change in strategy.) Even performance indicators may be misleading when used to judge management mindset. Executives have a way to rationalize deteriorating performance with broad economic trends (recession, slowing demand), local conditions (high interest rates, increased regulations), transitory issues (production mishaps, quality issues), sun spots, evil spirits, whatever—just not their strategy. That does not apply to new CEOs, of course. So start from a working hypothesis that the company is satisfied with its strategy, and that no radical changes will take place (until a crisis hits and the executives are forced out). Then look for signs of discontent to *disprove* this hypothesis.

There are exceptions. Grove's redirection of Intel from memory chips to microprocessor is a legendary example—but then, Andy Grove was a truly legendary leader.

Several elements from the Four Corners Model and the neuroscience research can help managers answer this question. Management's assumptions is one critical element, but so are existing goals (vis-à-vis performance), the company's self-image (as seen from its culture, its creed, its beliefs, and value system), its capabilities compared with market trends (especially technological), internal unanimity regarding its strategy, the hiring and firing of key figures, the recent performance of executives in charge, his or her public statements regarding the company (or business unit), and the way others describe this executive (ambitious? in the running for a top job? nice guy? ruthless?).

Answering Question #1 focuses the predictions: It tells the team whether or not to expect major moves or reactions or incremental moves/minor reactions.

Question # 2: "What Are the Competitor's Hot Buttons?"

Porter talks about hot buttons in the sense of what will provoke the competitors' strongest and most effective retaliation. He mentions emotional issues, strong beliefs, sacred "cows" (for example, attacking Microsoft's Operating System). The neuroscience basis for hot buttons is clear: Under the effect of strong emotional states or powerful drives, research shows that people make myopic choices. Understanding what type of situations will get the competitor "hot" can save a company form making a bad move.

Beyond the sage advice of avoiding moves that can evoke out-of-proportion reaction, the usefulness of understanding competitors' hot buttons is in its predictive power: We can state, quite confidently, what moves the competitor is *certain* to make (if provoked by our moves).

Answering Question #2 relies on intelligence in the drivers' corner, as well as strategy corner (which geographical markets are important? Which products are considered key to future growth? Which cash flows are critical?). Looking at what capabilities the competitor seems to focus on can give a clue as to its hot buttons. And again, it is essential to try to understand management's assumptions about where the industry is going, and which areas are critical to the company's growth. From neuroscience we know that personal attachments of executives will play a major role in the way their companies will react, so rationalization is of secondary importance. If the executive in charge of the division you are competing with made his first career moves in the product, segment, or country you are targeting, his emotions will have stronger effect than an objective cost-benefit analysis would show. To judge by the psychophysical research, he might never get to the cost-benefit calculations.

Question # 3: "What Are the Competitor's Blind Spots?"

People are good at convincing themselves (and then others) that what they would like to happen is what will happen. These motivated cognitions are especially prominent in the hierarchical structures of companies, where a powerful manager can mobilize significant resources and does not need the approval of others. Blind spots represent obsolete assumptions, ineffective practices, and wishful thinking beliefs that are kept alive by powerful executives or powerful corporate culture and creed, against market evidence that they need to be dumped or at least radically adapted to a new reality. Answering this question above allows the team to predict, with high certainty, what moves the competitor will *not* make, because it does not see the value in these moves or it is stuck in a position where such moves will have consequences *it does not want to face*.

Identifying a competitor's blind spots is the highest form of intelligence analysis. *It requires a more realistic assessment of where the industry is going than the competitor's analysis*. Recall the Industry Imbalance analysis at the beginning of this chapter. The competitor's executives are continually discussing "industry's issues." But do they see the disequilibrium tendencies, the pressures being built up under their feet? Identifying competitors' blinders allows, in the next step of a war game, to design moves that deliberately take advantage of competitors' denial and ignorance.

The concept of blindspots is consistent with the Schumpeter and Kirzner's view of the market as in disequilibrium state, where ignorance and error allow more alert companies to profit. Consider IBM and Dell. Back in the early days of Dell, IBM was capable of easily squashing the small company, which began its meteoric rise as a reseller of...IBM computers. IBM never bothered to block Dell. Later on, as Dell thrived on its direct-sale model, IBM failed to respond forcefully with a similar approach because it was wedded legally and otherwise to third-party distributors (so called resellers). IBM faced very high *trade-offs* in switching to a direct-sale model.

However, these trade-offs were not insurmountable, as evidenced by the IBM direct-sale initiative, which started in 1998. By then, Dell was the undisputed leader of PCs in the United States, with sales of 18 billion dollars and earnings twice as large as all of its major competitors combined. What stopped IBM from responding to Dell was not the existence of trade-offs but a *blind spot*: IBM did not believe that customers were sophisticated enough to prefer direct sale over the help of a reseller. Or in a more recent example, consider Ticketmaster, for 30 years the leading seller of tickets to all major events in the United States. It missed out on the emergence of a secondary online resale market (where tickets are auctioned by their holders), which started with Internet upstarts, and has been dominated by StubHub. In 2007, StubHub snatched Major League Baseball's resale business from Ticketmaster. Ticketmaster's assumption has been that its wide distribution and presence will keep other parties from trying to sell tickets themselves. Yet the resale market was just the *beginning* of a trend brought about by the ubiquitous Internet. In 2008, concert promoter Live Nation, which accounted for 15 percent of Ticketmaster's business, announced plans to sell its own tickets in 2009.[9]

Identifying blind spots require three steps:

1. Performing industry imbalance analysis.
2. Identifying a competitor's *corresponding* management assumptions and beliefs about the market.
3. Comparing 1 and 2.

1. Performing Industry Imbalance Analysis

Porter's Five Forces model of industry analysis is the starting point, coupled with the identification of weak signals of growing imbalance in the industry players' power. Unlike equilibrium models, we do not look toward what the new or higher power balance is going to be eventually. That state may never occur, and, as explained earlier in this chapter, it is a theoretical state at that. Instead, we look for trends that are changing the power of one or more players. For example, as the status of physicians declined due to social changes (more educated population with wider distribution of medical knowledge, wide availability of information on malpractice and medical errors, the rise in the credibility of once maligned alternative medicine, and so forth), and patient groups have been gaining in power due to legislative and political trends (the rise in patients' "bill of rights" since the mid-1990s), innovative drug companies pioneered the Direct to Consumer (DTC) medical advertising, by lobbying the FDA to change its regulations. By 2005, DTC advertising was already a $4.2 billion industry. No one would have considered DTC in pharma companies if physicians' bargaining power was not declining.

2. Identifying a Competitor's Corresponding Management Assumptions and Beliefs About the Market

In order to conduct a blind spot identification analysis, the team needs to conduct an industry imbalance analysis *from the competitor's management perspective*. In other words, think of it this way: If you were a fly on the wall in the competitor's executive meeting room, and the competitor senior management was performing an industry ("five-forces") analysis along the lines of task #1 of this process, discussing important trends affecting the various players, what would you have heard? To gain an insight into a competitor's management assumptions, one needs to look no further than public speeches given by the competitor's executives, in which they express their beliefs about where the industry is going. Additional sources of insight can come from looking at the competitor's strategic initiatives and "reverse engineer" them. Why is the competitor doing what it is doing? What does it reveal about the competitor's assumptions about what are, and what are not, the critical "success factors" in the industry? Additional details can come from examining service policies, advertising, want ads, and even political contributions (if not done as a collective by the industry association). These can give hints to the competitor's beliefs about what matters to buyers and what will matter to buyers in the future, as well as how substitutes and rivalry are going to evolve.

3. Comparing 1 and 2

A discrepancy between the results of step 1 and the results of step 2 is a potential blind spot of the competitor's management.

The astute reader will immediately identify an underlying assumption of mine that the industry analysis performed by a team is superior—in the sense of more accurate and less blind sided—to the same analysis if it were to be performed by the management of the competitor that this team is role-playing! In other words, say a war game is carried out in the photographic industry, and a team role-plays Kodak. My strongly worded claim is that the team's analysis of the photographic industry's structure and its evolving imbalances will be superior to the same analysis if carried out by Kodak's top management. (I have no intention of singling out Kodak; I will make the same claim, with the same certainty, about any company: General Electric, General Motors, or General Dynamics, to make a simple generalization.) The reason for this outrageous claim is that the team members (role-playing a competitor) are mostly middle managers, who are, by default, less biased than senior executives, and closer to market realities. Their analysis of industry trends and evolution of structural imbalance therefore tends to be more objective than the senior management of the competitor (or, to that effect, their *own* senior management as well). One of the implications of the neuroscience and behavioral economics research cited earlier is that middle management is not as personally encumbered by the implicit and non-accessible influences of history, emotions, biases, and commitments of the competitors' executives. The reasons are that middle management is more detached, less publicly involved in the industry's future, and less prone to self-persuasion. If you think about it for a moment, and take into account the inaccessible influences affecting competitors' executives as they think about the industry's future, and their more optimistic and self-delusional nature discussed earlier in this chapter, this is not as outrageous as it seems at first glance.

And it is born by the dozens and dozens of games I ran during more than two decades.

The astute reader will note, perhaps reluctantly if he (or she) is a senior executive, that the conclusion I reached in the previous paragraph, which is based on both a large body of evidence and anecdotal experience with numerous Fortune 500 divisions, holds true for *one's company* as well, not just for competitors. In other words, middle managers in a typical Fortune 500 company have a more realistic view of the industry and its changing nature of pressures than their bosses' bosses' boss.

That is why I call for war games to return to their roots as REALISTIC, which you may recall, meant accessible to managers at all levels in the organization, not to senior executives only.

Bringing It All Together

Assuming the team answered questions 1–3, it is ready to bring all the analytical and behavioral strands together for the main objective of a war game: predicting competitors' *most likely* moves.

Obvious vs. Most Likely

People tend to confuse "most likely" with "obvious." The two can be continents apart. *Most likely* prediction relies on insightful and careful intelligence analysis of competitors' observed behavior as well as underlying influencing dynamics. *Obvious* is the easy solution thrown up by managers who play a guessing game based on the first thing that comes to their mind.

Here is an example of how a combination of strategic and behavioral analysis allows you to move beyond the "obvious" or trivial, and into accurate predictions. Say a competitor just hired a new CEO. An obvious analysis (favored by so many "experts" in the press) will suggest that he is likely to institute changes in the company. This is trivial. A behavioral analysis will add several layers to this obvious prediction:

- If the new CEO is from outside the industry, he will most likely bring over whatever worked for him before (that is, his "success formula"). Bob Nardelli, a former CEO of Home Depot and an executive who grew up at GE, was hired by Cerberus, an investment firm, to lead Chrysler, which Cerberus acquired from Daimler Corporation. Following his arrival in August 2007, he swiftly instituted his Home Depot formula: Squeeze suppliers and get rid of poorly performing ones (Home Depot has been famous for that), pare down the number of models (Home Depot carries only a few major brands in each category), and consolidate the retail outlets (in this case the dealers) so that only the best-performing stores are left standing (again, the Home Depot store model). Moreover, the press was quick to note that Nardelli accomplished all these changes at breakneck speed, which is what he learned at GE, where the mantra of his former boss, Jack Welsh, was that slow change is like peeling a bandage slowly.

- Eventually, formulas for success tend to run into their limits, as there are things you just can't import from another industry. The new CEO will most likely then be stymied, blame everyone for his failure, and exit quickly.

- If the new CEO is an insider, the changes may appear less radical (it will not be a new "business model" mantra), but they will follow the pattern of changing directions from the former CEO. The reason is that the new leader lived a long time under the shadow of the boss, and accumulated a lot of frustrations while suppressing his visions and executing his boss's. When Charles Prince took over Citigroup from his mentor, Sandy Weill, he set out on an ambitious (and ultimately failing) strategy to turn the behemoth into a unified company rather than the strongly independent fiefdoms whose internal rivalry Weill cultivated. Prince also embarked on a radically different acquisition strategy than his boss, who was famous for giant deals. Prince advocated a string of small "pearls" approach.[10]

↦ A new CEO who was spurned from the top position is his company, and stayed in the industry, is most likely to be the most aggressive new leader, having a strong need to prove to his former bosses that he was the right choice. Jamie Dimon, who was in the running to become Weill's successor and who was dismissed in 1998, took over Bank One. With an aggressive—so aggressive it became legendary—cost-cutting and unifying campaign, he made the once-incoherent Chicago-based conglomeration of more than 100 acquisitions into a humming efficient machine—exactly what Prince was not able to do at Citigroup. He then sold it to JP Morgan Chase for $58 billion, to create a strong rival to Citibank.[11]

To recap: At this point a team already assessed a competitor's state of mind regarding the need to change course (first question), the opportunities and threats it tends to discount (blind spots), and the moves it will surely make if provoked (hot buttons). The results are some boundaries on the Moves space (the space of all possible moves). With this narrowed-down space, the teams find it easier to make accurate predictions, with the help of the final technique, creating a character, described in the next chapter.

Playing the Host

In every war game, one team plays the host. What does it mean to predict the host's moves?

It means giving the war game participants a sense of where management stands, what its main assumptions are, what the planned initiative means in the context of the company's overall strategy, what management's hot buttons are, and what the probability is that it will consider modification to its strategy.

However, the most important role of the team playing the host is to accurately and courageously answer these questions: What is management missing out there? What are our blind spots regarding competitors?

The analysis and exposition of the host's blind spots is the game's most valuable and yet most dangerous role. Pointing to the "elephant in the room" is a tough challenge. In its defense, the team should point out that, if it does not address blind spots, it is leaving the exploitation of those in existing or new competitors' hands. In looking at business history, for every large blind spot of an incumbent regarding an industry growing imbalance, new competitors were waiting on the sideline to gain profitable entry and wreak havoc on the management sleeping at the wheel. Wal-Mart exploited Sears, JCPenny, Montgomery Ward (remember it?), and other dominant retailers' blinders regarding the model of everyday low pricing. Starbucks exploited the belief of restaurant and food chains that coffee was an after-thought. John Mackey of Whole Foods exploited the grocery giant's assumption that expensive organic food is a fad for the rich only. Amazon exploited brick-and-mortar book retailers' deep convention that people always prefer to shop away from home, and see and feel the merchandise. Southwest Airlines exploited the full-service airlines' assumptions that all people value full service on every flight. And so on and so forth, from the beginning of time when the first entrepreneur looked at an industry dominant players and asked, "Why are they still doing *that*?"

So, in the end, predicting what your management will or will *not* do is as important as predicting what competitors will.

Chapter 4

Competitors as Characters

There are numerous methodologies aimed at helping a company make the best choices in a competitive situation, when it does not know the other players' intentions. Decision tree calculations and real option theory are just two examples. Game theory is another. These methods suffer from a debilitating lack of realism (for a more detailed critique, see the appendix to this chapter on page 86). Instead, try the following technique: Get to the essence of competitors by understanding their character.

Characters

The most central element in film and stage acting is building a believable character. Starting with a script, the actor needs to bring the character to life. Quite often the script does not provide enough data to answer every question the actor may have about the character. So actors must use various techniques to fill in the gaps, just as participants in a war game must do to role-play a competitor. Without becoming actors and actresses, what can managers learn from the techniques used by actors to prepare for a part?

Actors prepare for a part by spending days, weeks, and sometimes years doing research, and talking to people who know something about the character they will play. Managers must do their research. *If nothing more, a war game is a great catalyst to push managers to actually research their competitors, rather than rely on their anecdotal, personal experience with them.*

This research is easier than you think, and does not involve any trade secrets. Chapter 9 details the type of research questions to pose and the type of sources who may be able to answer these questions.

In the majority of cases, the research preceding a war game is carried out by either a competitive intelligence professional in your firm or an outside vendor. However, even with the best research in the world, you would still have to "complete the picture" by using role-playing techniques. No research is going to give you the full sense of a competitor, and how it is likely to behave in the coming months or years. You need a bit more help to get under the skin of a competitor. As unlikely as it may seem, you can actually benefit from studying how Hollywood goes about making characters that millions of people find credible.

How Did Al Pacino Play *Scarface*'s Tony Montana?

There are various acting schools of thoughts that teach different methods for using one's imagination in living the life of a character. When it comes to applying some of these techniques to business war gaming, we'll ignore the fluff and egos (and acting "theories" are full of both), and focus only on *what can be useful in a war game.* (I apologize profusely to devout followers of one method over another if I treat the difference in their gurus' teaching as less than world-shattering.)

Actors' training in the United States can be traced to the methods introduced by Constantine Stanislavski and his students, Lee Strasberg, Stella Adler, and several others. Until Stanislavski introduced his "system," actors were supposed to alter their voices and use dramatic gestures with every sentence; characters were grossly exaggerated. Stanislavski was the first to replace theatricality with realism. The central theme of modern techniques is believability, which is based on the "truth of the character." But how do you know this "truth"? Take a little tour with us of the elements that made Tony

Montana in *Scarface*, a movie where Al Pacino played a drug dealer immigrant from Cuba. Al Pacino is neither Cuban, nor has he ever been a drug dealer. There are four elements to getting under a character's skin (their order does not matter):

1. **Use a "Magic If."** The "Magic If" allows the player to live in situations he has never been in. On a psychological level, the word *if* gives permission to be something the actor was not: *as if* he was the Prince of Denmark (yes, Hamlet).
2. **Use the "Magic If" within a script, a plot, or a story line.** "Magic if" alone is undisciplined, so you use it within the play "circumstances." The actor is not Hamlet, but *if* he were a 30-year-old prince pondering the essence of life while approaching a castle where his uncle murdered his father and lives with his mother, how would he feel? These circumstances are likely to arouse some feelings in the actor. According to Stanislavski, applying one's past experience to the circumstances transforms the actor from playing himself into servicing the character.
3. **Look for a "theme."** To help the actor act, as in the character doing something on stage, acting teachers teach students to look for a theme, an overall objective, which propels the character throughout the play. For Hamlet it was revenge.
4. **Use sense memory.** If the circumstances coupled with an overall objective do not seem to raise any deeper understanding inside the player, because the circumstances are too far from the player's experience, actors sometime turn to a technique called sense memory. The actor activates remembered emotions from his past. Recalling the physical sensations associated with those particular memories can be helpful in this recall.

Let's bring it home to a war game. You have researched a competitor. You have some basic data about it. You are seated in a room with other members of your team, and have to answer: "What will it do? How will it respond to our moves?" Try the following:

1. I like to start with the competitor's overriding goal. The competitor's theme may be to remain number one in volume (market share) at all costs (even though its executives may trump profitability to appease analysts' ears). You can ignore a lot of inconsistencies in a competitor's actions, because you can safely predict that, at the end, *everything* will lead to trying to stay number one.
2. Use the "Magic If." Seasoned managers have been through a lot of experiences similar to what their peers at the competitor are going through. Now if you *are* the competitor, and you have this overriding goal, what would you do? How would you act?
3. Add the "script." The intelligence briefing (Chapter 9) gives you some material about the competitor's circumstances. Porter's Four Corners Model takes the raw data and creates a background for you to do your "Magic If." Don't just say, "If I were in the competitor's situation, this is what *I* would do." *The lesson from Stanislavski and Al Pacino and any other actor or actress, who completely and utterly convinced you in playing someone else is an attempt to lose the "I."* Say, "If I am the competitor, and these are my circumstances—limitations and constraints, drivers and capabilities—this is what is consistent with this character."
4. Bring in some relevant sense memory. If it does not help, it can't hurt. It makes you think outside

your immediate circumstances. For example, if the war game calls for role-playing a competitor under intense competitive pressure and managers facing possible layoffs, picture yourself in a similar situation, even if it was your first summer job at McDonald's. Try to recall the physical circumstances of that time. Where did you hear about the possibility that you may be fired? What did you see when you heard that? The physical circumstances may make it easier for you to feel the emotion. That will make your own experience work in the service of the character's circumstances (in this case, a competitor's managers facing layoffs).

There are several other techniques to try and "feel" like the character/competitor. Students of Stella Adler, another teaching guru, were taught to use their imaginations, not their personal pasts, to get *in* character. Underlying Adler's technique is an intriguing assumption, which participants in a war game can use for their own benefit: Adler believed that inside each of us are endless numbers of characters and that at each moment in our daily life we construct and *play* a particular one. Therefore character work is simply a self discovery process. As she put it: "You are everybody. In some area of your life you are a killer, a crook, a liar, and a whore. You are a genius, a god, and pure."[1]

Adler used some "tricks" that I found very useful, though naturally a bit dramatic. Used correctly (that is, with moderation) they can bring all the competitor data together into a clear focus. Here are two that I used and found especially constructive:

1. Imagine competitors as animate or inanimate objects that remind you of their character type. I found these a terrific vehicle to convey a competitor's essence and "personality" without going into unnecessary

tactical details. The character can be an animal (a bull, for example; see Chapter 10 to see how "bull" describes an aggressive, rigid competitor).

2. Use a stereotype (rich playboy, high-tech geek, stumbling, wounded giant, and so on), which helps quite nicely in the "purifying" the essence of a given competitor. Though this simplification process may seem a tad less realistic than the complexity of real-world characters, as long as one adheres to the circumstances (provided by competitors' intelligence brief), the simplification actually works to cut to the core and reduce white noise in predicting a competitor's reactions. Applying this technique in role-playing a competitor, one may ask: "What does it mean to be a proud market leader whose leadership is challenged severely?" (Answer: The stumbling, wounded giant can still cause a lot of damage by his sheer weight and foggy coordination.) What does it mean to be a Japanese executive in an American setting (proper, reserved, disciplined, hierarchical, impatient, in a less-formal and a lot more self-centered culture)? How would a French entrepreneur-playboy think about his "little" venture ("I am on my yacht today; don't bother me")? Where would a CEO who rose through sales place his emphasis? (It's not strategic planning, we know that!)

U.S. managers (it less so in Europeans) are careful not to use stereotypes, as it is politically incorrect. Yet the stereotypes we use are not derogatory; they serve as an excellent organizing vehicle. Their utmost value is in culling the tendency to dwell on the secondary issues.

Consistent with the use of constructive stereotyping, Adler further believed in focusing on what she called the deeper voice—the essence of the character. We find this advice very insightful. So ask the following question, as you analyze and grapple with competitor's data: What is the *deeper* voice? What in the company or the executive's past—culture, upbringing, and experiences—will have the deepest impact on current thinking? For example: What do we know about Chinese culture and the way it affects Chinese executive thinking and their relationship to others in the world? Does Confucius's teaching have any bearing on business strategies? If I am an Arab executive, running an investment fund for the king, what do I take from my culture that will always influence my behavior? Arab culture places honor as more important than other qualities. What actions will I deem offensive to my honor?

Sometimes a deeper voice may be a traumatic experience. GE perceives itself as a master of business in which it owns the assets and in which huge economies of scale are at work.[2] Accordingly, it will think several times before committing another mistake such as acquiring subprime originator WMC (a business where GE did not control the underlying asset). GE lost $400 millions on this deal, but, more importantly, it was out of control, an antithema to the *control-obsessed* environment of GE.

Although managers tend to get lost in statistical data (mostly publicly available) market share, revenue growth, share of advertising voice, and other technical and tactical numbers, they miss out on actually capturing the essence of their competitors, which (in our experience) yields much better understanding and *therefore* predictions. This is especially true in technical industries such as pharmaceuticals and high tech, where excessive reliance on technical data, such as IMS's data on the number of prescriptions fulfilled, or the technical specifications of a new product, mask the market realties. It is not surprising that, in those industries, many carefully constructed plans do not survive competitors' responses. Stella Adler would have sent these executives to "spy on people, studying their character elements....”[3] As she pointed out to her disciples, including such famous actors as Robert De Niro, Marlon Brando, and Elia Kazan, “Acting is hard because it requires not just the study of books...but constant study of human behavior.”[4]

Good advice for many executives I have met, and many more MBAs.

Strategy Analysis and Competitors as Characters

Though most managers would find it hard, at first, to take tips from Al Pacino seriously, my suggestion is to just try it! Business schools teach the neoclassical rational decision-making approach to management,and students are accustomed to think of business as impersonal sets of spreadsheets, and to ignore or dismiss “irrelevant” personal influences on companies’ behaviors. The mafia Godfather’s cliché, “it is business, not personal,” clinched this myth. However, as Bossidy and Charan observed, the *personal* has a crucial effect on decision in most organizations.[4] Therefore, when sitting in the breakout room having to make sense of the rims of data about a competitor, give our *heuristic devices* a try. If they don’t help, move back to your comfort zone!

Appendix:

The Shortcomings of Game Theory and Other Mathematical Approximations of Human (Competitor) Behavior

If your management is currently in love with game theory (or some other mathematical modeling technique *du jour*) you may be intimidated into using it in war-gaming decisions. It is not an effective tool for you. (Feel free to copy and send this appendix anonymously to the executive who seems to be the present advocate of the technique, or similar mathematical approximations of real competitors' behaviors.)

Starting with defining payoffs, which are hardly known in advance in the real world, continuing in the contrived construction of the options available to each player, and ending with the assumption that choices will be made rationally, game theory suffers from lack or realism in approximating (and predicting) competitors' behavior.

For our purpose, though, game theory can be useful in demonstrating the *limitations* of mathematical modeling in general, and the strengths of behavioral models in predicting competitors' actions. Have you heard about the Prisoner's Dilemma? It is the most celebrated case demonstrating the power of game theory, so let's take a (critical) look at it.

The Prisoner's Dilemma (PD) assumes that two suspects, A and B, are arrested by the police after a robbery and that the police have insufficient evidence to convict them. So, the prosecutor offers each of them a deal to testify against the other. If the other remains silent, the one who confesses goes free and the silent suspect receives a 10-year sentence. If both remain silent, both prisoners receive one year in jail for a lesser charge. If both confess, each receives a five-year sentence.

	Prisoner B Stays Silent	**Prisoner B Confesses**
Prisoner A Stays Silent	Each receives one year in jail	Prisoner A receives 10 years Prisoner B goes free
Prisoner A Confesses	Prisoner A goes free Prisoner B receives 10 years	Each receives 5 years in jail

The dilemma arises because the outcome of each suspect's choice depends on the choice of the other, but each prisoner must choose *without knowing* what the other suspect has chosen.

If this situation seems somewhat contrived (where is the judicial side in all this?), hang on. It gets worse quickly. Realism in game theory is altogether a secondary issue. The PD demonstrates a mathematical situation (equilibrium or stable solution) in which *individual* rational choice—maximizing an individual's outcome (which means minimizing his sentence)—is a dominant strategy but not optimal for both players (*collective* rationality). To see that, try to follow this reasoning, which the suspects are *expected* to follow. If you knew the other suspect would stay silent, your best move is to confess, as you then walk free. If you knew the other prisoner would confess, your best move is to confess, too, because, if you stayed silent, you'd receive 10 years! The other suspect reasons similarly, and therefore also chooses to confess. However, the joint confession leads to each serving five years, whereas if both stayed silent, both would have served only one year! The PD situation then demonstrates that stable states need not be in the best interest of the players, but that is the solution they will gravitate toward! In mathematicians' lingo, PD demonstrates that in a non-zero-sum game (where one's win is not another's loss), a Nash Equilibrium (stable solution without a possibility of improvement) need not be a Pareto Optimum (best collective outcome).

Hey, wait! Where are you going? It gets better!

What is wrong with this famous game theory prediction of human behavior? A few things. First, game theorists apparently did not hear of Omerta (the criminal code of staying silent *no matter what*). Second, they never heard about guilt or innocence and the ability of defense attorneys to save even murderers from going to jail, regardless of testimony of partners. Third, if you believe the example, changing the payoffs (years in jail) will automatically guarantee a change in criminal behavior. Do you buy that simplistic approach to behavior modification? Even Skinner would not have. Fourth, even the limited experimental studies carried out on this contrived "game" done in a controlled setting of college students in a lab showed that 40 percent (!) of the players behaved differently than this theory predicts. (They stayed silent.) Fifth, imagine how the theory will perform in complex, real-life strategic choice situations (with many more players, with uncertain outcomes, and with choices that are *not binary* [confess, don't confess]) but that include *substantive* creative elements, if it is so unrealistic in this very simple game.

But put all that aside. The biggest weakness of this theory is that it assumes you can't reliably assess the other side's moves and/or you can't think more than one step ahead. If you could predict that your accomplice will not rat on you, no matter what, the theory predicts that you'd *still* chose to confess, because you then go free.

"And live the rest of my life in fear of retaliation when he gets out of jail?" you are thinking. "No, thank you. After all, there are some *characters* you just don't mess with, you know?!"

So, we need a more realistic approach to competing and planning: An approach that allows us to assess third-parties' character in a reliable way. As the anonymous writer of a Wikipedia item on the Prisoner's Dilemma confesses: "In deciding what to do in strategic situations, it is normally important to predict what others will do."

War games, after all, are about normal business life, not mathematical elegance.

Part III

Step-by-Step

Chapter 5

Step 1: Is It Time to War Game?

The Basic Requirements

Chapter 1 posited several situations for which war gaming is a superior planning tool. Let's expand on those in a bit more detail. Use a war game if:

- You need to draw a plan or decide on a strategy.
- The success of the plan depends on the real-world moves and countermoves of competitors (and other third parties).
- You don't have *direct* information on those intended moves.
- You don't want to just *make up* hypothetical assumptions about what competitors' can do.
- You are not interested in a theoretical modeling of the market but in predicting what competitors are *most likely* to do to your plan so you can "competitor-proof" it as much as possible.
- A planning failure could be costly to you and the firm.

If I had to make a bottom line statement here, it would be: Be honest with yourself. If you are confident you already know what competitors are going to do, or how they are going to react to your strategy, don't bother with a war game. Similarly, if you are *committed* to going a certain way *no matter what* competitors will do, there is no point in playing war games either.

Common sense goes a lot way toward saving money.

Which Plans Call for War Gaming?

- Meeting a change in market conditions (so-called Landscape games; see the next section).
- Launching a new product or service.
- Entering a new market.
- Increasing share of a product/service
- Reviving a brand.
- Defending against a new competitor or against a growing threat of lower cost substitutes to your product/service.

Fundamental questions answered by all war games are:

- What will competitors do?
- How can we outsmart them?

Applying these two questions to the previous list of plans means you are looking for deeper insight on such problems as:

- How is the market most likely to shift in the next three years, and how can we meet these changes better than competitors?
- How do we increase market share in our current markets without giving up the store and starting a price war?
- What is the best way to launch our new or improved product/brand against tough competitors?
- With what do we replace our current product when its life is over, and stay ahead of the competition?
- What is the best way to enter the Brazilian (Chinese, Israeli, Indian, Hungarian, and so on) market?
- How do we defend against new entry of molecules EL2043 and Pf7077 into our market? (This isn't a joke; it's pharmaceutical company lingo. That's the way they talk!)
- How do we take back the leadership position in this segment against competitors who are bigger, better financed, and better positioned in customers' minds?

↦ How do we maintain our product leadership position against the rising power of low-cost Chinese manufacturers?

It should be clear: *You may not like the answers*, but war games are the most realistic setting to place these questions on the table before going to market, and perhaps losing your shirt because of poor planning.

1 Limitation

The only limitation on simple, low-cost, transparent war games is that they should be focused on one industry, or one set of players at a time. That is due to the fact that the war game methodology I advocate places the realistic role-playing of a set of third parties at their center, as the means of gaining superior perspective. If these parties change, one needs to do a different game. For example, war gaming the competitive landscape for a software package aimed at IT professionals, and another software package aimed at consumers will require two games, even though the competitors my be the same! The reason is that, if you bunched these two packages together, you would still need two different industry imbalance analyses, and two different strategies. So, in effect, you'd be running two games. Similarly, launching a new drug applies to a particular therapeutic area but not to another. The reason is that disease areas quite often differ on patients, physicians, alternative treatments, and, well, competitors (*some* will overlap, but not all). Therefore, if you have two industries, play two games, building, role-playing, and making predictions for different *characters* each time.

Which War Games Are Appropriate?

Once you determine the decision/situation that calls for war gaming, you have to select the type of game to run. There are basically two types of games: games for formulating a new plan (Landscape games) and games for testing an existing plan (Test games). Selecting the game's type is quite simple because, to a great extent, the situation itself determines the choice. You either have a plan already, or you don't. The two types of games differ slightly in the flow of things, but otherwise both answer similar questions:

Landscape Games Answer	Test Games Answer
What will competitors do?	How will competitors react to our plan?
How can we outsmart them?	How can we "competitor-proof" our plan?

Landscape Games

Landscape games are so named because their objective is to examine the "competitive landscape." These games are designed to enable management to place the company in the most advantageous position given *anticipated* future market conditions.

Companies do not examine the competitive landscape unless there is an urgent sense that that landscape has been changing, or is about to change rather drastically and *unfavorably*. Without that "sixth sense" among managers—which is not a sixth sense at all, given all the early warning signals thrown up by the disequilibrating trends—plans are drawn assuming a continuity of competitive conditions ("We know what competitors *can* do"; "We expect distribution to continue to consolidate"; and so on). When there is no sense of a seriously changing environment, managers invest most energy on internal considerations (political, operational, and perhaps historical), which always trump external focus.

During the period that management believes the market is relatively stable (or is in equilibrium in "economist speak") management is more vulnerable to the Absolute Performance fallacy, the "Strategy in a Vacuum" syndrome. The competitive landscape is considered a known quantity with no surprises, and marketing or advertising research tends to replace strategic thinking about outsmarting competitive dynamics. A manager drawing a plan is prone to naval gazing. What are the *available* resources and capabilities? What is the existing position with distributors? What are the features of the product or service, and the marketing message that best fits that product or service? Considerations of some hidden, ambiguous, and changing market preferences are naturally swept under the rug. Underlying the plan is a belief that competitive response is *containable*. The manager seeks confirming evidence that the plan is *good*, and advertising agencies and the habitual large consulting firm are more than happy to provide soothing "intelligence" in the form of a lot of statistics, histograms, boiler templates of market research, historical anecdotes, and so forth.

Alas, if *company-centric* naval gazing analysis of needs and capabilities in the market were enough, not one strategy would ever fail to deliver, companies would always meet their goals, and Wall Street would always reward them with rising evaluations. So what goes wrong?

Simply put, the problem is that the market is never at its hypothetical equilibrium, and "stable states" are misleading. Under-served customers, over-served customers, and customers' changing needs present disequilibrium opportunities, and entrepreneurs and incumbents alike make moves that, *in retrospect*, reveal the illusion of market equilibrium. This is why

Landscape games are so important. Landscape games are aimed at unmasking the underlying, ambiguous changes in a market early on. In the process, Landscape games unmask competitors' adjustments, or lack thereof, to the emerging disequilibrium risks and opportunities, and lay the foundation for a strategy that meets Porter's definition of *superior* strategy: a set of activities that create a *unique* market position that can last longer than the next quarter.

Landscape games are best played when management wants to stay ahead of the changing market. Jeff Taylor, founder of the Internet-based job-search giant *Monster.com*, called this approach the "second curve"—a beautiful term, because management is typically already on top of the next curve issues, but the "second curve" is hidden. Landscape games are favorites of new managers, who need to chart their territory and design a plan to strengthen the company's position.

Case Study

Landscape Game

Landscape games are sometime known as early warning games, because companies who play them are proactively looking at weak signals and trying to interpret ambiguous changes in the market. This example deals with a war game ran by an insurance company that prospered by targeting a segment in the market over-served by other, much larger insurers. Over-service is a little-appreciated, but quite-prevalent phenomenon in many markets. It occurs when market players offer the buyers more than the buyers want, and charging high prices accordingly. If the buyer has no alternatives, she may elect to stay out of the market completely.

In the insurance market, insurers offer a huge variety of plans for catastrophic events: health, disability, life, property, and so on. The common thread of these plans is that they charge high premiums (especially the healthcare plans) but in return offer high benefits. The insurance company in this case found a profitable niche in this market: It served customers in the market who were able to pay little, and it return expected less; that "less" was still better than *nothing*, to tide low-income people over until they could get back on their feet.

There are several examples of companies that profited from over-served markets: Ikea in furniture (selling self-assembly at much lower prices), iTunes in the music industry (selling single tracks rather than whole CDs), and Dell (if you are knowledgeable, give up the handholding reseller). Companies that offer over-served customers a lower pay–lower service choice play an important role in consumer welfare.

The insurance company in this case had no direct competitors, mostly because the business was too low-margin to attract other insurers. It made money by having its entire set of activities tied closely with the target market. In other words, this company was doing only what made sense in light of the product and the buyer. No one could run a tighter ship or tighter chain of supporting and reinforcing activities aimed at providing exactly what it said it would: low-cost, lower-benefit insurance product.

So why run a Landscape game? Because management wanted to make sure it was not missing out on strategic risks and opportunities in the market.

The game yielded two interesting findings: One, the biggest risk to this company was government intervention. State and federal government regulates insurance products heavily. If government mandated certain benefits to be offered, the market would disappear. Consider the effect of a mandate to purchase of a whole book, if all you needed was a paragraph.

Second, the game revealed a slow but persistent push by managers throughout the company at raising the level of frills. Whether it was more bells and whistles in the customer service departments (unnecessary for the company's typical customer), or offering more sophisticated/expensive products, this natural managerial drift toward an "upgrade" of operations would have resulted at the end in a serious undermining of the whole strategic concept of the company. One result of the war game was an internal campaign to explain the company's strategy to all employees, reinforcing the notion that more is not always better.

Through the years, I've seen many Landscape game reveal that the strategic risk is not from external developments, but from *watering down* a company's strategy with inconsistent activities.

■■■

Test Games

Test games test an already developed strategy against the likely responses of competitors (and, at times, customers, potential alliance partners, government or industry regulators, distributors, and so forth). These are by far the most popular types of war games, because the time line of decisions in most companies is more suitable to formulating strategy by a product or brand team and then testing it closer to implementation. Also, the sad truth is most companies are not proactive.

Case Study

Test Game

A software company, the global leading vendor in its area of specialty, spent millions of dollars and several years developing an application that extended its product line into an unchartered territory. The first version met with little success in penetrating the market. Several months before releasing the second version, the application marketing team ran a game to test its premises about the market, and to find ways to reach its target market, where competitors were much stronger.

At the time that the game was conducted, one of the company's rivals was being acquired by a larger software company. That was the first indication of the turmoil this market was to endure during the next few years. The significance of this early acquisition did not escape the participants. During the game, the issue of market consolidation came up repeatedly. The implications of that disequilibrium trend were critical to the company's attempt of market penetration. If it had difficulty reaching a new audience before, the anticipated consolidation (participants identified prospective acquirers, which in retrospect proved "on the money") was going to make things worse.

During the game, it became clear that the plan was not focused enough to allow the application team to reach its market share target. The company lacked the credibility of its competitors to approach a different set of decision-makers. Its sales force was not fluent enough with the type of cases that could demonstrate to the potential user the power of the application. The cost of the product was high, in accordance with its sophistication, but without expertise to demonstrate its superiority over competing products in improving decisions, clients would have little incentive to shell out a premium for its high-powered features. Ironically, the game also revealed that the company's managers themselves did not use this sophisticated product, although it was supposed to add significantly to their ability to identify new prospects in the market! As a result, the company embarked on a training initiative to better equip its salespeople, built convincing case studies, and changed its lead generation process to focus on its large body of existing loyal followers inside companies' IT departments.

■■■

But What if They Do *X*?

In Chapters 3 and 4 I presented a combination of methodologies from economics, decision sciences, neuroscience, and acting aimed at answering a simple question: What will competitors do? Some experts advocate techniques aimed at answering a different question: What kind of surprises can competitors pull? What if they do X?

War games testing a plan along these lines typically dream up a basketful of "worst-case" contingencies. This is a mistake. Companies should work on developing rapid *response* capabilities, not plan against all contingencies in advance.

I am not saying, "Don't test your plan against a worst case." You should be weary, though, of "worst-case" war gaming becoming an academic exercise in thinking about *all* possible disasters. Such an exercise fails one of the 7 Tests: It becomes unrealistic. Similarly, it's easy to suggest that people "think outside the box" about competitors' responses, but most battles for market share take place *within the box*, and the art of war gaming to a large extent is defining successfully what this box is *for a competitor*. Planning against *X*, which in actuality is out of character for a competitor, may sound good, until one considers that such "contingency" plans must divert scarce resources from more pressing issues of *likely* reactions, and, worse, diffuse strategic focus. Hannibal won the battle against the much-larger Roman army because he predicted their *most likely move*, not because he planned against *everything* that could go wrong!

So, No Testing Against Surprises?

By all means, test against unexpected responses within the context of exposing blind spots in the host company's thinking. The "unexpected" surprise is not from a competitor's perspective, but the host's! Strategic surprises are almost always enabled by blind spots of the company being surprised.

Executives can be quite blind to events under their noses if they do not conform to their views of the "right strategy." For example, in 2005, when telecom/wireless company Sprint acquired wireless carrier Nextel, Nextel had the most loyal base of business customers in the cellular market, not the least because of Nextel's IDEN network, which allowed for a very popular "push-to-talk" feature. A year later, the Nextel network approached capacity, and quality of service deteriorated fast. Instead of increasing the network's capacity, Sprint moved the subscribers to its network, which was incompatible with their phones, and did not have the popular push feature. In addition, Sprint dropped the Nextel name and began using the Sprint name, which was better known among consumers, not businesses. By 2007, Sprint's shares lost 60 percent of their value; Verizon and Cingular (AT&T) were eating its lunch. Such a "surprise" reaction from customers was only surprising to Sprint. A good host team in a war game should be able to point at this elephant in the room.

Chapter 6

Avoid Potential War Gaming Traps: Bad Timing, Unreceptive Management, and Insular Culture

Bad Timing

Test failed: # 2

1. It has to be Realistic.
2. **It has to Empower.**
3. It has to be Accessible.
4. It has to be Lots of fun.
5. It has to be Inexpensive.
6. It has to be Simple.
7. It has to be Transparent.

Test # 2 of any war game you decide to run is that the game must empower you to *walk away from a bad plan*.

Don't run a war game when its outcome can no longer change anything. If the deadline for launching a new service is February, running a war game in January means that most of the tactics are already in place: The advertising copy has been written, the promotion mix has been discussed with distributors, the marketing communication message had been prepared with the help of the PR firm, and production deadlines have been agreed upon. (Whether or not they will also be adhered to is another issue altogether.) So what is the point of a last-minute game? A war game is not a practice "dry run" or a dress rehearsal. Dry runs and dress rehearsals can be done with the product or project team only, going down a checklist making sure each and every member knows his or her role. War games are aimed at finding out how the plan stands up to competitive reaction, not how it stands up to its own checklist.

Games that are run too close to D-Day are typically confirmatory, "feel good" games. I can fully sympathize with a nervous brand director who wants to make sure everyone is on board with the plan. But my experience shows that war games that are confirmatory may end up less so than expected, or more so than needed. If it turns out to be a cheerleading occasion, you wasted time and effort, and gained little. If it turns out the participants played faithfully and poked holes, what should the hapless sponsor do if it is five minutes until midnight? By rule, few corporations allow a manager to walk away from a plan where a team spent months preparing, and when its deadline is looming. Delays do not bode well for funding, even if the delay may mean saving millions. Delays do not bode well for careers, even if the delay shows prudent judgment. This is corporate life.

I've seen games that were run too late produce ill feeling in those involved. The initiative team—whether a product, market, or project team—resents the fact that its long nights and hard work were being attacked. The resentment yielded defensive posturing rather than a helpful discussion.

Competitors' teams feel uncomfortable attacking their peers, with whom they had to work later on. If the plan could hardly be changed, what is the point in criticizing it?

Decision-makers, if present in a late game that is "turning south," may witness a drop in morale, and they hate that. Executives want a unified, enthusiastic team behind the plan. Naysayers and negative comments at five minutes until midnight may be honest, but honesty is not always at the top of an executive's agenda.

Of course, it is always possible that a last-minute game reinforces the team's concept and produces a consensus regarding the plan's exceptional merits. We all like those games, but when you are thinking about putting together a game, think not about "it would be nice to have everyone on board with my plan," but rather "what if we need to make major changes? What if the plan falls apart?" If the war game will not empower you to walk away from a bad plan, don't run it. There are other formats in which a team can come together for a cheerleading session. An office party comes to mind. Maybe an outing?

So, do yourself a big favor: Save the money and effort of all those who are trying their best to help you, and do not run a game too close to a deadline. You would know what "too close" means; just ask yourself: Can I still walk away from a bad plan?

Unreceptive Management

Tests failed: # 1, 6, 7

1. **It has to be Realistic.**
2. It has to Empower.
3. It has to be Accessible.
4. It has to be Lots of fun.
5. It has to be Inexpensive.
6. **It has to be Simple.**
7. **It has to be Transparent.**

War games are tools to be used directly by managers who need to plan and then execute. But these managers have bosses, who have bosses. Bosses are typically talented, bright, able people, but some may not be comfortable with the idea of an open role-playing of the company and its competitors.

Running a war game where the decision-makers are present in the room, either as participants or as observers, and are not comfortable with an open, honest, and at times "politically incorrect" debate (for example, when it comes to exposing blind spots) is anything but simple. One needs to maneuver around their sensitivities. The result is often an unrealistic game, because confronting an unpleasant reality may meet with resistance. If there is a wide divergence between senior executives' assumptions and beliefs, and the perceptions of their middle and field managers, senior executives may at best dismiss middle managers' analysis, or express frustration and anger. Either sentiment is unproductive. Furthermore, if senior executives' different perspectives are based on information not available to participants, the game fails a third test: that of transparency.

"I'm disappointed in your job performance. It's been ages since you've brought me an innovative idea to ignore."

Unreceptive management can be classified into several types. Each type requires a different approach to handle, but don't expect miracles.

Thin-Skinned Executives

Some research suggests that, as one climbs the corporate ladder, the ability to face criticism diminishes.[1]

"Loyalty and enthusiasm are the two things I value most in an employee. You're hired!"

Thin-skinned executives with sensitive egos who participate in war games are a rarity. Most just stay away. However, when they are part of a game, the game is useless, and at times it can turn ugly. It is irrelevant whether or not the executive is correct, and the game participants are wrong. The result is the same even when the tables are turned.

There is no optimal method to overcome such an obstacle. One should, as a rule, try to avoid inviting executives who are known to be thin-skinned. Many are smart enough to stay away on their own. However, if the executive insists on taking part in a game (okay, maybe he is not that smart), one trick I learned through the years is to place such an executive on a competitor team. In this role, the executive needs to identify his own company's weaknesses. Few will do it, and even fewer will do a good job, but at least their damage can be *somewhat* contained.

The best advice is still to not invite these people. War games are aimed at people who are actually doing the planning and will have to execute the plan, not at their bosses. Trying to keep it "in the family," so to speak, with coworkers who attempt to help, is an important consideration to keep in mind. Let the ego-sensitive executive participate in one of the large-scale, computer-generated, million-dollar games run by his cronies from the large consulting firm. Chances are that no one will ruffle his feathers there.

Neurotic Managers

Some executives who lack self-confidence, or are new to their positions and have a strong fear of failure, may want a game to go exactly as they envisioned it. Any deviation—a discussion that focuses on a "wrong" blind spot, a strategic option that is too "radical"—may cause these sponsors to become nervous.

It is actually hard to watch the inner conflict of these executives, as they try to keep a fake "open mind" while seething inside. On one occasion, I felt as though I was watching a wounded horse, and all I wanted to do was put that poor manager out of her misery.

If you find yourself running a war game with a boss exhibiting the signs of neurotic discomfort, it is highly advisable to call a break in the game, preferably at a natural break point (between teams' presentations, for example), and ask the executive what his or her concerns are and how can they be remedied in the time remaining in the game.

Addressing the neurotic boss's needs does not serve the realism of the game, but it is a simple act of humanism. You know the "undesired" results of the game will be suppressed by the neurotic boss, anyway, so have mercy.

The alternative is to run the game as honest as it should be, and then resign. On the occasion mentioned a couple paragraphs previously, that was the outcome of a game. The manager who organized the game then found a better position.

Domineering Bosses

At times, bosses are overeager to participate in the game, and their type-A personalities find the role-playing of market confrontations to be a wonderful outlet for their competitive nature. These executives are the opposite of the thin-skinned and neurotic sponsors, in that they actually contribute greatly to the game, and feel very comfortable with an open debate. The problem is that, if their style is aggressive enough, they will dominate the game to a point where others' perspectives and analyses will get suppressed.

If the game is run with an outside facilitator, you can only hope you recruited a person with a strong personality to reign in on this type of executives. But if you run the game yourself, what do you do? You cannot risk your career by trying to keep the executive from dominating the discussion.

My advice? Invite another executive to the game who can balance out the aggressive one. Place the second executive on an opposite team. Let the two battle it out. At least that way, the game will be effective, even though it may fail Test #4: It may not be a lot of fun for the participants, who will find themselves playing second fiddle. On the other hand, sometime it actually *is* a great fun to watch two ambitious, smart, competitive and powerful senior executives duke it out under the excuse of a role-playing competition.

The plan, rest assured, will only improve after such a high-powered hand-to-hand combat.

Insular Culture

Tests failed: #1, 4, 6, 7

1. **It has to be Realistic.**
2. It has to Empower.
3. It has to be Accessible.
4. **It has to be Lots of fun.**
5. It has to be Inexpensive.
6. **It has to be Simple.**
7. **It has to be Transparent.**

Sometimes a company's culture can work against an effective game. There are many ways in which culture can prevent a game from effectively presenting and exploring market reactions or from improving on the existing plan with better strategic options:

- A **"not invented here" culture** will prevent strategic options from being superior. As teams present and debate what to do to outsmart competitors or "competitor-proof" a plan, solutions will be confined to old and tried conventional wisdom. I've seen these outcomes fail especially with smaller companies going against market leaders.
- A **"harmony at all cost" culture** will prevent discussions from pointing out blind spots and will confine confrontation to polite exchanges. Though teams do not need to be *impolite* to each other, having to watch out continually not to offend anyone creates games that are complicated and unrealistic. They are also not fun.

- A **paranoid culture** will prevent transparent discussions. Paranoid companies are worried about many things; legal issues (such as anti-trust), leakage of information about their plans, and sharing competitive reviews with too many employees are just the tip of the iceberg. Discussions are then stunted mid-sentence.
- A **cynical culture** will treat any discussion during a war game as useless. "We've seen management zigzag, restructure, and reorganize too many times to think the results of this game are going to have any effect." "The only ones who management listens to are the large consulting firms, so why bother?" And so on.

There is no panacea to handle these and other cultural obstacles. However, the simple, straightforward, and honest game recommended in this book should acknowledge these issues, put them on the table, and work with or around them. Yes, companies are political animals, not everything works as it should, management might be conservative, indecisive, or both, but, in the end, the people who plan and execute are not VPs or SVPs. They are product managers, brand directors, project leaders, and marketing managers. They need to produce and execute the best possible plan given all the constraints listed in this chapter. My war games are for them.

Chapter 7

Step 2: The Teams—Who Do We *Not* Invite?

Once you decide to call a war game, and be sure you're avoiding the potential traps discussed in Chapter 6, the next step is to create the teams.

Note: The following rules of thumb apply to games lasting between one and one and a half days, consistent with the need to keep the game inexpensive and accessible to middle managers. Most professionals and managers cannot afford to take two whole days away from their desks.

Rule of Thumb #1: The Number of People in a Game Should Be in the Range of 12–48

You can run a small, intimate, "family-only" type game, with members of your team and a few additional experts from other departments. Or you can decide to run a larger war game to drum up *political* support, by inviting key people from around the organization. Although I have run war games with 100 people, I do not recommend very large games. Running too small a game is also counterproductive; you need a critical mass to energize the room, and bring some new external perspective to your plan.

Rule of Thumb #2: The Number of Players per Team Should Not be Less Than 3, and No More Than 8

If you decide to run an intimate, "family only" game, your best option is to role-play a maximum of two competitors and your company, a total of three teams with three people per team. The "golden rule of three" is based on the need to break a tie if two cannot agree on an issue in the analysis and strategy rounds of the game. The reason I recommend a maximum of eight people per team is that, with more than that, some participants are passed over during breakout discussions for lack of time, and that does not help your cause.

Rule of Thumb # 3: The Number of Teams Should Not Exceed 6

You can play a game with as little as two teams: your company and one competitor. Or, you can play against multiple competitors. However, the number of competitors that can be effectively role-played is no more than six. The game's methodology calls for ample time for each team to role-play a competitor in front of the room, sharing intelligence analysis and understanding of the opponent's character. Each team needs a minimum of 20 to 25 minutes to do a good job in conveying the essence of the competitor's character and its likely moves. In a typical one-day game, which consists of two rounds, this constraint implies a maximum of six teams, *including* the host. (See Chapter 10 for an hour-by-hour rundown of a real game.)

What if We Have More Competitors?

Not a problem: Use strategic clustering and create a *composite profile* (see Chapter 8). The fact is that realistic war games (unlike computer games) do not require move-countermove iterations for a large number of competitors, because a company never faces equal threats from every one of its potential rivals. There is never a strategic need for an in-depth understanding of *all* of its rivals' characters. Time spent on irrelevant competitors is time wasted. The tool of strategic clustering enables an efficient role-play of a large number of competitors without a waste of time.

■■■

Who to Invite

- Your team, of course.
- Other people in the organization who have experience facing these competitors in other markets or knowledge about competitors' characteristics.

If possible and practical:

- Competitors' former employees. (Beware of never asking them for proprietary information. They can contribute significantly to understanding the competitors' *character*, though.)
- People whose support you need in order to accomplish the plan's goals.
- Representatives of other functions with whom the plan should be coordinated for execution (production, legal, R&D, and so forth).
- People who have good knowledge of additional third parties in your market, such as customers, distributors, and regulators (according to their relevance to your situation).

Who to Invite Selectively and *Cautiously*

- Advertising agencies. Caution: The advertising people working with your team or with corporate can be self-serving and amazingly insular. They live in their own world where advertising reigns supreme, even if in the real world it is just a marginal factor in performance. Invite those who are older and more seasoned, as they have passed the need to use too much MBA-laden hype.

- Research vendors. If the intelligence you used in the game came from a research vendor, it may be worthwhile for the researcher to take part in the game. Get the researcher, not the boss, so that you have firsthand perspective.
- Customers. You may include internal people with knowledge of the customers, or decide to bring in a live specimen. A trusted customer can take part in the first round of the game when teams role-play competitors and share their analysis. A customer's perspective can be of enormous importance in creating realism in the game. However, remember that the home team is asked to expose your company's blind spots. Are you comfortable with a customer listening to that?

Who *Not* to Invite

You may think this is less important than who to invite, but it is not. Inviting the wrong people can ruin a good war game!

- Easily offended people. Politically correct types should stay away from war games.
- Shy people or people with a fear of speaking up. War games call for managers to express opinions, take sides, take on a character, and join a debate. People who sit by the side and doodle do not contribute.
- Very junior employees. They typically belong to the second group.
- Loud and over-aggressive people. It may not be their fault, but booming voices and a tendency to get too excited tend to suppress a productive debate.

- The people in this picture. They are not *fun*.
- Senior executives who are thin-skinned, neurotic, or domineering. (See Chapter 6 for details.)

Team Composition and Balance

There are several factors behind a success of a game: good intelligence, rigorous frameworks, and, naturally, the quality of the teams. There is no magic formula for creating a quality team. If you choose your people based on the characteristics provided (outspoken, passionate, with a sense of humor, who can take it as well as give it) you'd probably be okay regardless of team composition. But some guidelines from my experience should help.

Even though I recommend the use of several techniques from great acting teachers, it does not mean you should be looking for managers with acting talent. My interest in "acting" is confined to techniques and tricks that help a team understand a character as true to life as possible with a limited amount of information ("script").

So who should you place on the teams? That depends on two factors:

1. What is the goal of the game? At what level is it played?
2. Is it a competitor or a home team?

Size Matters

There is a natural correlation between the goal/level of the game and its size. Games that are played to pressure-test business unit strategy, at a global or regional level, are by nature played with more participants and at a higher level. These games run between 30 and 50 people, and the mix of the people should approximate the guidelines set here for an optimal mix of field, staff, function, and expertise.

Games such as testing a launch plan or a plan for deeper market penetration (taking away share from a competitor), or defense against a new threat at the product level are more tactical in nature (or more focused on one product strategy), and can be played productively and effectively as an intimate, almost "family-only" game at the brand or product level, with a few reinforcements from other areas in the company. "Family games" typically run with 12 to 20 managers. These games do not need to achieve an *optimal* mix, as long as they bring some experience from outside the core members of the planning team.

Competitors' Teams

The rule is to strive for diversity of perspectives and experiences, but it is a flexible rule. Do whatever you can, and do not think that, because/if you did not achieve an optimal mix, the game is lost. The quality of the participants overcomes many hurdles, including lack of diversity. Diversity is enhanced with:

- Staff and field managers.
- Various functional skills.
- Experience and knowledge of the external environment.
- Different personalities.

By default, most war games are populated by more marketing managers than other disciplines. The bulk of participants come from the product, brand, or project team that is responsible for executing a commercial plan, and these are marketing professionals. Our crusade to take war games out of the exclusive domain of large-budget senior-executive simulations and make them accessible and inexpensive is the result of seeing the need of *marketing managers* for an effective tool for their unenviable job of sending a product or service into a hostile environment. The good news is that marketing managers bring unparalleled enthusiasm, vision, and creativity into any game. The bad news is that marketing managers can use a *reality check*, or what Chris Howell, a war game moderator at Cadbury Schweppes, calls *practical* ideas. So, whenever possible, add a few participants who can bring additional practical considerations—for example, people who visit customers daily and fight the street battle with competitors (salespeople), people who are supposed to meet the set production specifications (operations managers), and people who listen to customers' complains or quiz customers' needs on a regular basis (service managers, customer service managers, and market research professionals).

It is advisable that *someone* in the game asks, "How much would it cost?" before recommending additional advertising or price promotion, so you may want to include one finance or budget analyst. In some more strategic games, teams can use the benefit of a scientist or a technologist who is intimately familiar with the strengths and *limits* to the company's R&D. Given these few checks and balances, marketing managers can carry the day, lead the teams, and infest everyone with their energy. They are a delight to work with.

One tenet I do recommend strongly is that that each team includes a competitor expert—whether the company's competitive intelligence manager, a former employee of a competitor, or a manger who faced the competitor in another market or region. At Cadbury, managers are given the responsibility of traveling the globe and learning about ways Cadbury won against competitors in various markets and regions. P&G has managers called Business Insight Managers who bring the best ideas that worked *against these competitors elsewhere in the company* back into the war games.

The competitive expert is charged with a hefty and unique responsibility: keeping the discussion rooted in facts and data.

As Stella Adler preached in her legendary acting classes, acting is giving life to a character within the play's circumstances. She called it "Commitment to the Circumstances," and each game should have at least one individual whose role is to vigilantly bring the debate back to this practical commitment.

Personalities

Though the team majority will be made up of hardworking, dedicated, and toe-the-line managers, each team should have one "troublemaker." If you can't find enough of those, and some companies weed them out quickly, at least place one troublemaker on the team of the competitor *that frightens you the most*. Troublemakers are managers who are less conforming than others, who passionately advocate an unpopular position, who may obsess about a specific issue, and who stand up to group think and team pressure even at a cost to their career. You know who they are. Troublemakers exist in every company. They come in different shades and colors: a scientist who believed in powdered electricity, a VP who remains a rebel (as rare as this is), a near-retirement engineer who for 15 years cried wolf.

Bring these individuals into your game. They can turn a run-of-the-mill game into a strategic or tactical breakthrough.

The Home Team

You should put courageous people on the home team.

Recall the home team's task from Chapter 3: The home team performs a blind spot analysis of the company's plan, or the company's existing strategy, checking it against the disequilibrium tendencies they identify in the market. Depending on the company's culture, this can be both unpleasant and risky. To accomplish its goal, the home team should do what Col. Van Riper did to the U.S. military in the Millennium Challenge 2002: show its cracks for everyone to see.

The role of the home team is to bring an objective, *market-oriented* perspective to the plan. For that, the home team may have to be, at times, ruthless and, at other times, supportive. If the plan is bad, it must identify its blind spots one by one. If the plan is good, it should not file nuisance complains against it. Most plans are neither totally off nor totally on mark. Blind spot analysis is therefore not an easy task. Managers tend to fall for the more obvious "weaknesses" in a plan such as running against an entrenched competitor, or having a smaller budget than desired. Those risks are all given, and well known to management.

The home team should leave the obvious to the competitor teams who are going to have a field day exploiting obvious weaknesses. Real blinders are not that obvious, and are rooted in obsolete assumptions deep in the company's consciousness, about industry dynamics and their future evolution. The team members should have an ability to look at the market and see subtle, ambiguous, weak signals of change on the customers' side, the power of substitution, or other rising imbalances that may have been missed by the planners, and that will come to bite the company later on. They should be able to see patterns that are not on management's agenda. Given that management is smart and well informed, this is not a task for the weak of heart or the conformist of thoughts.

And then the team must make its case as succinct, honest, and practical as possible, knowing it has to live with the others in the room for years to come.

As I said previously, find your less-timid people for the home team, and brief them beforehand. They should understand their task well before accepting the assignment.

Who You Should *Not* Put on the Home Team

Try not to put the core members of the team that worked on the plan on the home team. Remember the role of the home team: bring an objective, market perspective. The core members of the planning team (such as a brand team, product team, market team) who invested many hours devising the plan cannot look for its blind spots (if they could, the plan would have not had any!). Even the most open-minded product managers or directors will be on the defense if asked what's wrong with their plan. The core members, *especially the leader of the planning team*, should be assigned to the competitors' teams.

Where Should You Put Decision-Makers?

You don't have to have senior executives in your game. If you do, however, here are a few rules of thumb:

- Put the most senior person in the room on a competitors' team, typically the largest (or most pressing) competitor. That ensures that the role-play of the competitor will be done with gusto.
- If the game sponsor is a very senior executive, such a general manager or president of a division, or the company's CEO, and he or she expresses an interest in playing, put them on "jury duty." As a "juror," the senior sponsor has the privilege of asking questions throughout the game, but, unlike a judge, cannot insist on a particular answer. If the senior sponsor does not want to attend the whole game, but still wants to show support, I recommend that he or she make the opening remarks and then be present for the last round, when teams make recommendations for improvements in the original plan.

The reason for not including a senior sponsor as a player is that, under most cultures, the team members will find it hard to disagree with the leader's analysis. Even if the leader is the exceptional individual who is a democratic, nurturing, and affable leader, it is hard for his team to disagree with him, and for other teams to attack his analysis.

If the senior sponsor insists on actively being on a team, and you are unable to convince him otherwise with the experience-borne explanation, place him on a competitor's team, and very gently request that he make everyone on his team express his or her perspective even if it contradicts his own.

An exception: Sometimes, having the senior person play enables young, bright stars to shine, as they (respectfully) show the boss their strategic skills. It really boils down to who the leader is and how well he leads. But then, isn't it true of leadership in general?

Senior-Executives-Only Games

Having a senior executive or several of them in a game can bring energy and credibility to a game. Have too many senior executives in a game, however, and it comes similar to the sport of polo: unclear what all these players are doing and why they are on the field—but they get to show how well they ride.

Executives-only games fail Test #1 of Effective War Gaming: They are unrealistic. Realism comes from a wide range of perspectives, expressed honestly and openly, and those are brought by middle managers and field managers who deal with customers, competitors, suppliers, and distributors on a daily basis.

So stay away from games *saturated* by high-powered people. Let the large consulting firms make millions off them.

Summary

Suggested Teams' Composition

- Bulk of participants: marketing managers (including market research) plus competitor experts (competitive intelligence managers, insight managers, KM managers, former competitors' employees).

Augmented by (depending on size and level of game):

- Sales managers, operations people, a finance analyst, technology/R&D managers.

And always try to include a troublemaker or two!

Team Leadership

It is not *necessary* to have a pre-designated team leader. In a game where senior executives participate, they assume a leadership position by default. Those who are really, really, good leaders refuse to take over this role, in an attempt to encourage others to voice their views. However, team dynamic makes them the leader de facto. So you might as well tell them they are in charge of the team.

When the game is a "family-intimate" game, without a clear boss on a team, teams assign "leadership" roles naturally to the first person who takes charge. That natural process is as effective and as productive as pre-assignment. *So let it happen.*

Team Facilitators

Depending on the size of the game, larger games call for more structure of the teams, including team facilitators and/or scribes. At times the team leader is the team facilitator as well. He or she will sum up the discussion at critical junctures and make sure the essential points are captured on a flip chart or electronically. If the leader is a senior executive, another member of the team may have to take over the scribe role. At any rate, one person on the team, or an outside secretarial help, *must* capture the team's notes for both presentation and record. This is very important: Don't let the team's discussion be lost to cryptic notes or messy flip charts. Make sure one person writes it in legible and descriptive bullet points, so a summary can be later released to the participants.

Chapter 8

Deciding Who to Role-Play

Which third parties in the company's environment should you role-play? Management must decide which competitors they'll be playing. Ninety-nine percent of the time the choice is self-presented. But maybe you want to look at more than the obvious alternatives. Here are a few suggestions regarding the selection of the right competitors, and instances where role-playing other, non-competitor players in one's market can be productive. Finally, what do you do when you have too many competitors to play?

Which Competitors Should You Role-Play?

Quite often, the choice is obvious. Sometimes there is only one competitor, which is a target of the marketing plan, so you don't need to agonize over whom to role-play. If there is more than one competitor who is relevant for the plan on hand, most companies tend to role-play their largest rivals—those with the highest market share in their segment. They also instinctively tend to include a competitor that is owned by a large parent company, even if it is not currently a dominant player in this segment. This is not totally capricious: Competitors with large market share in your segment have a stake in defending it, and they will throw resources and use their entrenched networks in blocking your move. A smaller competitor owned by a deep-pocket conglomerate should be monitored closely for possible corporate investment, which may turn it into a threat, or a sale, which may turn it into even a bigger threat. In short, the obvious competitors are easy to identify.

There are two situations, though, that call for a bit more sophisticated approach. First, role-playing only the dominant players may mean missing out on an emerging threat, which can turn out to be worse than the familiar ones. As Bethlehem Steel and Microsoft can attest, it is the threat that you don't see that is going to give you the biggest headache (think mini mills and Google). Second, if the market is a contentious one, with several roughly equal players and no dominant one, how do you choose who to include and who to ignore?

Strategic Grouping

In his book *Competitive Strategy*, Michael Porter introduced a tool that can help exactly in those situations. He called it strategic groups or clusters. He defined a strategic group as "the group of firms in an industry following the same or a similar strategy" along a set of several strategic dimensions.[1] Sharon Oster, in her book *Modern Competitive Analysis*, added the following requirement: "Strategic groups are defined as clusters of firms within an industry that have common *specific assets* and thus follow common strategies in setting key decision variables."[2] (italics added)

In other words, based on the history of the industry, and the pattern of early investments in assets (choice of focus on production vs. marketing, or a bet on specific technology), firms with the same early choices tend to follow similar strategies in such areas as diversification (or focus), pricing, geographic scope, product mix, customer segmentation, cost, vertical integration, and so on. Those firms can be looked at as belonging to a strategic cluster. Some industries may have several distinct strategic clusters (the automobile industry, for example). Other industries may have none. In the automobile industry, GM, Ford, Toyota, and several others rely on a broad line of products to capture volume, share platforms, and benefit from economies of scale, which allows them to price their cars lower. Based on their similar assets and strategies, they can be grouped together into one cluster. On the other hand, Porsche and BMW belong to a different cluster, with a narrow product line and lower economies, and they use differentiation on performance and technology to price their products higher.

Strategic clusters can be quite stable through time, if they are protected by high barriers to entry. If the barriers are high, profitability may differ widely between clusters in the same industry and firms may not be able to jump from a less-profitable cluster to a more-profitable one. If barriers are low, clusters are much more fluid. In the automobile industry, Porsche and BMW are, on average, more profitable than other companies. However, one does not see GM becoming a sports car specialist, nor does BMW try to sell automobiles in every segment and every market. The reason is that clusters have barriers (called mobility barriers) that can prevent easy switching back and forth. Brand name, technology, distribution, and scale are just few examples in the above industry.

The importance of strategic groups is their effect on how their members react to change in the environment. Members in a group tend to react similarly to an external industry event, and differently from members in another cluster. There's the concept's value in selecting competitors to war game.

Overall, rivalry is stronger within a strategic group than across groups. In other words, competitors in your cluster should be the first ones to be included in your war game. The reason is straightforward: Competitors in your cluster use a similar type of assets and similar strategies to go after the same customers you do!

That said, it is worthwhile to examine your cluster's barriers and other clusters' barriers to get a feel for possible moves in the industry. A competitor in another segment may be acquired by a new entrant with technology or distribution that may allow it to expand into your customer base (for example, Oracle's acquisition of Hyperion, which extended Oracle applications to Performance Based Management.) Or a big player may decide to play in all clusters (think Wal-Mart entering organic food). If your cluster is more profitable than others, you may want to examine strengthening the barriers in a war game. If another cluster is more profitable, you may want to examine its barriers to see if they are coming down.

Who Looks Like You?

Before you war game, draw a quick and intuitive map defining the clusters in your industry based on major strategic differences, not tactical moves. Who seems to use the same strategies as you? Who is perceived by customers as similar to you? Those are your most pressing competitors. As you'll see, you may still elect to select a representative from other clusters, but your first choice should be direct competitors. In the laundry detergent industry, for example, there is a cluster of marketing-oriented firms that created brand-name products by investing in advertising and innovations with a cumulative effect through time, and a cluster that relied on investments in production economies and produces generic products without any marketing investments. These are large strategic choices that are based on specific assets and investments. The two clusters do not compete directly. They may not even sell at the same channels. The buyers are different. If you were P&G (Tide, Ariel), you should select Unilever first (Wisk, All) and store brands second.

The purpose of your map is not to be accurate but to allow you a quick selection tool. *Those who look like you, talk like you, and walk like you belong in your cluster, and they should be invited to the ball dance first.*

No Clusters? No Problem

If you can't think of strategic clusters in your industry, don't feel bad: You are in good company. It is not clear how many industries have distinctive clusters. One study in the United Kingdom from 1987, which looked at response to industry change, suggested that one-third of industries had clusters, because firms in those industries failed to show common response to industry dynamics.[3] That does not mean the other two-thirds did not have clusters; it simply means it is hard to estimate the number directly.

In those industries where firms' responses to change seem uniform, you may be witnessing what Porter called *competitive convergence*: firms employing similar strategies and only differ on operational effectiveness. The steel industry in the 1950s and oil-producing companies since the 1980s seem to offer good examples of competitive convergence. Large U.S.–based steel companies in the 1950s and 1960s employed similar technology (open furnace), offered similar range of products, and competed for the same customer segments (government, construction, ship building). Oil companies have been slowly but clearly imitating each other, competing on buying reserves, ceding innovative drilling technology to equipment manufacturers (vertical disintegration), and becoming mostly project managers and political negotiators.

Through exogenous shocks such as new technology, shift in demand, and/or government regulations some industries may split into more well-defined clusters (for example, the U.S. steel industry since the 1980s) and some will go the opposite route, as clusters and firms disappear, as in the pharmaceutical industry. United States steel producers started to split into distinct clusters as mini mills with electric arc technology spread and foreign competitors grew. Some producers diversified away from steel; others invested in new technology.

The reverse happened in the pharma industry. Whereas throughout the 1980s the pharmaceutical industry showed distinct clusters (based on branding and marketing, areas of specialization, and production efficiencies), there has since been substantial convergence as consolidation through a frenzy of mergers and acquisitions created copycat large pharmas with no distinctive strategic positions.

Pharma firms may still differ in their *size* due to historical reasons, but they all use the same model of one-stop-shop and vertical integration, organized as massive investments in the whole value chain of discovery, development, and marketing, building portfolios across multiple diseases while in each area surviving on (or dying with) a few *megabrands*, relying on central R&D facilities with declining productivity (GlaxoSmithKline being an exception), and using a failing sales model organized around key opinion leaders as drug endorsers and a drove of salespeople who try, more and more in vain, to get physicians' attention. Yes, Pfizer and AstraZeneca may do more marketing than Bayer or Lilly, but these have become tactical differences, or operational execution differences, not different strategies and asset base. All large pharmas are profitable based on *high* prices in the United States, and *lower* prices elsewhere. They all regard marketing as molecule-centric, not patient-centric. Even their executives all look alike, having grown in the insulated, high-margin, high-risk environment of chemical trial and error.

If you are in an industry such as this, selecting your competitors is a matter of tactic more than strategy. You know which competitors pressure you most in the market, which ones have the (temporarily) superior product or service in your segment, and which ones have the muscle to kick your plan's butt. No point in agonizing over whom to role-play. Still, a remaining issue is what if there are just too many of those look-alikes?

Composite Profile

If major differences between competitors do not exist, you can use two techniques to manage their numbers in a war game.

1. Select either one as a representative.
2. Select several, but assign them to the same team to create a composite profile.

A composite profile minimizes the differences between the competitors in the service of creating a sense of their character and, therefore, their likely response.

The instructions to the team role-playing several competitors together are to distill the common response and at the same time, if they find intriguing "outlier" responses that are more likely for one competitor than the other, just highlight those.

Composite profiles do not work as well as an in-depth analysis of one company, but remember that the essence is not accurate profiling of every competitor, but practical improvements to the plan. These improvements do not require accounting for every possible variation in response from every possible competitor. They do require capturing the essence of reactions from those most likely to prevent you from reaching your goals.

Role-Playing Other 3rd Parties

One of the best war games I ever played, which might have changed the fate of traveling by air, involved a team that role-played the customer (in this case, airlines). Actually, it was a composite profile team, playing several large airlines along the guideline of accentuating the common reactions, but also highlighting any outlier that should be reckoned with.

It turned out that customer team, which had one manager who used to work for a customer, and one manager who spent six months out of a year at the customer, offered invaluable insights as to how the customer saw the differences between the host and its competitors. This is exactly what a customer team does best: substitute reality where *internal* perceptions typically rule. You should think about the following example: When you and your team conduct a SWOT exercise (Strengths/Weaknesses/Opportunities/Threats), do you define strengths and weaknesses from a customer's perspective or from your company's?

Not every game calls for a team dedicated to customers. In most games, customers will be "represented" on each team by the market research professional, a sales manager, and so on. Customers' perspective will be considered and presented through the actions of competitors. However, if your company's sales are dominated by a *few large customers*, consider putting one team to role-play them.

The same rule applies to companies in industries in which the balance of power is tilted toward one or two major players, such as government regulatory body, a large distributor, or a dominant supplier. In these cases, consider a team devoted to role-playing this power broker. For example, pharmaceutical companies may at times want to play the FDA or Medicare/Medicaid. Toy manufactures may want to role-play Toys"R"Us or Wal-Mart (or a composition), because of its dominant role in determining industry's dynamics.

Consider these cases the exception, though. Most war games are about competitors. All other players in the industry—buyers, end users, suppliers, distributors, regulators—get their "say" through the analysis of these competitors' strategies, capabilities, goals, and management assumptions.

Chapter 9

Step 3: Intelligence and Then Some

You went through Step 1: deciding what to war game. You've done Step 2: deciding who to role-play and who to invite to the game. Your next step is preparing the competitor intelligence briefing.

A war game is the only method of developing strategies in which external information is *systematically* gathered and then used by participants to "get into character" of those they role-play in the game. Without good intelligence, there is no role-playing. Instead, managers gladly resort to mirror imaging: imposing their own biases and assumptions on others in the market.

A common misunderstanding about competitive intelligence is that it involves "trade secrets" such as competitors' actual strategic plans. This view misses the point of role-playing: If you already *know* what competitors' are likely to do, why run a war game? The whole value of a war game is that you don't have direct intelligence about competitors' plans, and yet you want to make the most realistic assessment of their future moves so you can prepare for them. The type of intelligence needed for a war game is about character, not secret plans, and it can be found legally if one knows what to look for. The third step in the process of running a war game is, therefore, for you, or someone in your company, to gather credible intelligence and prepare a briefing book for the game's participants to be able to role-play a competitor as realistically as possible.

This chapter provides guidelines (a list of information requirements) and, more importantly, lessons learned over the years about what works better in briefing books. It is surprising, for example, how little information is actually needed to make for good role-play. This is a short chapter, befitting my advice: Whatever you do, make sure the briefing book is

SHORT.

The Absolutely, Positively Necessary Information

Assuming you have read Chapters 3 and 4, you already have an intuitive understanding what information is required to do the analysis and role-play the character. You may find it useful to think about information as building blocks of a character. What do we want to know about a character?

- What are the character's age and background?
- What are the character's relationships with others and with the physical surrounding?
- What is the character's physical state of being?
- What is the character's emotional state?
- What does the character want?
- What does the character presently do?
- What immediate precedents caused the character to do this?
- How does the character perceive him/herself?
- What prevents the character from accomplishing his or her objectives (from within and without)?

The intelligence briefing is similar to a script, only with a business focus. Each of these tidbits used by actors to create characters is useful in analyzing companies. We just need to translate it into a business jargon. What we do in analyzing a company is not that far from how British actor Daniel Day-Lewis prepared to play an American oil prospector in *There Will Be Blood*. A good intelligence briefing gives the managers the *circumstances*, so they can build a believable character within them.

Team Briefing

Each team should receive in its packet whatever information from the following list you were able to gather on the competitor it has been assigned to role-play. You don't need to edit the information. It can be in the form of newspaper clips or Wall Street analysts' reports. It can be a summary of annual reports, or an interview with a customer. You don't have to cover every item on the list. It is better to focus on the dominant characteristics than dump data on everything. *You will find the task imminently easier if you think of the competitor data as clues to the competitor's character.*

- Where did it come from?
  - Competitor's history: Where did it come from, what has it succeeded in, where has it failed? Where are its roots? How has its focus changed from its earlier days?
- What has it kept from its past?
  - Competitor's culture: beliefs, values, philosophy, canons. "This is the way we do things around here."
- What is it doing now?
  - Product market position.
  - Relationships with distributors.
  - Relative strength with customers.
  - Strength of sales force, relative share of S&A cost, compensation of salespeople, their skill level.
  - Marketing approach: advertising, promotion. Advertising agency's typical approach.

- Production essentials: cost of production (comparative if available), scale, processing technology, capital equipment, plants capacity and flexibility, quality control, excess capacity, location of plants and unionization problems, access to supply of raw material, any proprietary manufacturing advantage.
- Research prowess: patent areas, basic research strength, speed of development, creative talent, alliances with academia.
- Financial ratio analysis (comparative to you)/overall cost position: Is it a low-cost leader?
- Depth of management: Are the young as good?
- Corporate overall portfolio strength. Do different areas support each other? Compete with each other for resources?

↱ What does it want?

- The competitor's stated goals (especially financial).
- Its real "bottom-line" expectations from the business unit, brand, or product you are up against.

↱ How does it think?

- Habitual Large Consulting Firms (HLCF) used by competitor's management.
- Executives' background (professional, personal, educational). Anyone parachuting from the HLCF?
- More important is to get *some* background on the executives you are facing with your product or brand than on the top brass at corporate.
- Internal politics: Who is influential? Who is rising? What camps are formed?
- Board composition and board-CEO relationships. Rubber stamp? Independent agendas? Wimps? Role models?

  - The place of the product/brand/business unit you are going against in the parent's company portfolio. Is it important? Is it a cash cow?

- How does it feel?
  - Governmental and legal actions against the company.
  - How is its recent performance (especially on growth, market share, profits, ROI, and share price) compared with past performance and publicly stated goals? Note: Graphics are much preferred over a windmill of numbers.

Even partial answers to these questions will provide your teams with ample material to supply clear predictions of competitors' future moves.

Group Briefing

Every team should get the same industry information portion in their packet. The industry portion is aimed at enabling the participants to conduct an industry disequilibrium analysis. So you are looking for clues for how things are changing among the major players in your market: the buyers, the end users, the competitors, the suppliers, the potential competitors, and the producers of substitutes looking to replace you.

Include in this portion *whatever is available* from this list:

- General articles from the business press (*The Economist* is by far the best, followed by the *Wall Street Journal*) on the industry as a whole.
- Wall Street analysts' reports on the industry as a whole.
- Trade magazine overview articles of the state of the industry and future trends.
- Market research studies and surveys about the consumer/customer statistics, characteristics, and emerging trends.

- Any news reports about acquisitions, mergers, entry by new players.
- Any significant data about supply chain: major supply trends (availability and prices), labor trends, and so forth.
- General articles about substitute industries and their trends (examples: alternative medicine as related to the drug you are war gaming, and wireless technology for a land line war game).

Sources

There are two types of sources for data on the competitors (and, to a degree, the market as a whole): human and published. They are also known as primary and secondary.

Almost all the information in a war game comes from published (secondary) sources. The human intelligence comes from:

- If you have the money, conduct some interviews with credible observers (academics, experts, customers).
- If you invited salespeople into the game, they have a lot of tactical primary intelligence on customers and competitors.
- Your engineers, scientists, and operation managers taking part in the game have some knowledge of competitors' production and R&D capabilities.

Pay Attention to What They Do, Not What They Say

Quite often, a company's communication with the outside world goes through PR firms and internal communications departments. The results are sterile, carefully massaged statements for public (and Wall Street) consumption. Call me an old cynic, but I just don't believe management public statements. That's why, when I read annual reports, I hardly pay attention to what the chairman says. I pay attention to what his company or its division or its product team has done. Actions speak much louder than sanitized communication. ***But,*** I do pay attention to how executives' tone *changes*. Reading annual reports' "Letter to the Shareholders" is fun if you do it over a few years to get a feel for what is transient and hype, and what the real strategic concerns and strategic views are that seem to surface repeatedly.

Pay Attention to What They Say, Not Only What They Do

The last section's rule of thumb has one exception. If a company says outrageous things, it is worth paying attention, as you can glimpse a character underneath. Here is an example: In 2007 car sales in the United States dipped to their lowest level in 10 years. Not since 1998 did automakers, *especially U.S. automakers*, sell so few cars. Here is what GM's Vice President Mark LeNeve had to say to *USA Today* about this sorry state: "[2007 will be] looked upon as a watershed year as the industry coped with globalization, record fuel prices and a shift from SUVs to crossovers."[1]

What do you make of this public statement? Watershed means turning point, a defining moment. The worst year in a decade is a watershed? Have any of the problems been fixed or are about to be fixed? Is globalization new? Is fuel going to become suddenly abundant? Is it a surprise that gas guzzler SUVs are falling out of favor?

No. Even though 2007 was not a watershed year by any means, and LeNeve's positive spin is just that—a *spin*—one can almost hear the real sentiment underneath, which is what a car wreck survivor would say, as he crawls out of the window and looks back: "Thank goodness it wasn't worse."

This is how I would analyze GM if I were running a war game about it. In this case, what GM says reflects what GM does: hope against all odds not to go bankrupt in the next 10 years.

Who Should Prepare the Intelligence Briefing?

The short answer is your market or competitive intelligence (CI) manager. If your company or business unit does not yet have one, ask yourself why, when everyone else has one. Second to a CI manager doing it professionally, one practical solution is to distribute the work among the teams. Each competitor team can be tasked with preparing its own dossier on the competitor using whatever public data it can find, using search engines, a clipping service, data bases, and a brokerage report secured from your investor relations department. It may not be as rich a script as a briefing prepared by an intelligence manager, but it is infinitely better than relying solely on anecdotal experiences of your team with these competitors. If you have a budget, you can hire an external research vendor to prepare the briefing. Just keep the vendor on a leash: A large brief is not better than a short one; it is just longer. To get a sense of competitors' characters so you can realistically predict their likely actions, you don't need more than a few pages of the *right kind* of information. Rims of numbers, market statistics, and technical data do *nothing* to enhance a war game, but will add significantly to cost.

Now you are prepared. It is time to role-play.

Part IV

Running a Business War Game

Chapter 10

Step 4: Let's Play! A Real Game, Hour-by-Hour

Game 1: Reviving a Brand

The Settings

This is a description of a real game, played in the early 2000s, modified to protect the proprietary nature of the host company's information. The industry gamed was beverages. The category within the industry was a drink product available in almost every home. The category was very profitable and large, with massive barriers to entry due to strong brands, sophisticated research technology, extensive advertising and marketing expenditures, and massive cost of distribution. Retail trade's shelf space is notoriously tight, and any newcomer will have to persuade the big retailers to take out someone in order to put its product on the shelf.

The category's dominant technology made research and development a significant determinant of competitive advantage in the marketplace. However, this advantage was always transitory, as competitors caught up sooner or later. The market leader has been a U.S.–based company that we'll call "LX" in this game.

The *host's* brand in this category (labeled "WP" in this game) has been steadily and slowly declining five years prior to this war game. It was still second in market share, but due to a recent innovation by the market leader, it was losing ground fast in every market but South America. A new global brand director has taken over the brand two months earlier. He was charged with developing a "revival plan" for the brand.

In discussions leading to the war game, the global brand director selected two more companies to role-play, in addition to LX and his own company. One was a European-based and European-focused company, which has been expanding slowly in Asia and has been trying to gain a foothold in the United States ("RR" in this game), and another U.S. company, which was a leader in a related food category, but had only a small footprint in this snack product ("D" in this game). It was unclear whether it harbored ambitions to muscle into this category with massive organic investment or acquisition.

The Plan to Be War Gamed

The global brand director and his team put together a "brand revival" plan that called for attacking the market leader aggressively and taking share away from it. The brand director needed to present his final plan to the Division VP for approval before implementing the plan.

The Game's Structure

The game called for four teams with eight managers on each team, for a total of 32 players. Teams were diversified both functionally (R&D, marketing, competitive intelligence, market research, manufacturing, finance, country managers, salespeople) and nationally (representative from Europe, the United States, Asia, and South America).

Game Type

Test game. The brand team prepared a plan and the game was called for to test it against market response. The plan outlined global directives that would inform specific regional action planning for the brand.

Team	Description	Global Market Share	Comments
WP (host)	A division of a diverse conglomerate	22%	Includes only 1 person from the brand team. All other brand team members were allocated to competitors' teams.
LX	Global market leader	35%	The global brand director was on this team, plus two ex-employees of LX
RR	European-based and -focused	12%	Included European sales people and a European country manager
D	Leader in another category, small presence in this category	5%	Included an ex-employee and an ad agency consultant with experience in that other category

Game Plan

Round 1: After a short presentation from the brand team, the four teams would break out to role-play competitors LX's, RR's, and D's responses to the brand team's plan. The host team would prepare its analysis of potential blind spots in the plan.

Round 2: The host team would be dispersed among the other teams. The now-consolidated three teams would break out to prepare improvements to the brand team's original plan, based on Round 1's predictions. These improvement proposals, in turn, would each be tested *live* in the room against the opposing teams, role-playing their assigned competitor.

Round 3: Having survived dynamic consistency tests (testing against competitors' *likely* reactions), suggestions for improvements would be examined for internal consistency (with the company's overall strategy) and external consistency (with the identified market disequilibrium). The surviving options would be consolidated into major themes.

Pre-game Preparations

Comment: Small touches such as a photo of the competitors' executives in charge of this category, a sample of competitors' products, and paraphernalia (competitors' logos, t-shirts, caps) help teams get in character. Use your imagination!

Hour-by-Hour Instructions (and Running Commentary)

8:00

Start the game by putting the existing plan on the table.

At the start of the game, a representative from the brand team went through a concise PowerPoint presentation of the plan, covering manufacturing, marketing, distribution and sales details, and market research assumptions underlying the plan.

Comment: This presentation brings everyone, including participants from other divisions and corporate functions, up to speed on the plan.

Highly recommended: Allow for clarification questions by those unfamiliar with the plan, but do *not* let this part of the game run into a full debate.

8:15–10:00

Introduce the methodologies. Remember: These methodologies work together to reach one goal: accurate predictions of competitors' likely moves.

For the snack game here, the following frameworks (reviewed in details in Chapters 3 and 4) were demonstrated to the crowd:

- Industry imbalance analysis.
- Porter's Four Corners Model.
- Blind Spots Analysis.
- The behavioral economic/neuroscience perspective.
- "Competitors as Characters" techniques and tips.

Comment: Don't worry about repeating what participants may have heard elsewhere (Porter's model, for example). Many participants do not have MBAs and those who do demonstrate B-School's greatest achievement: Once you receive your degree, you forget anything and everything you were taught. It's a survival mechanism for those joining the corporate world, where thinking is actively discouraged (except for the top team).

Highly recommended: Presenting the analytical frameworks is best done using a run-through example. The example should demonstrate analyzing an industry's disequilibrium forces and a competitor's character analysis. Many of those who did some training in B-School had only a theoretical discussion of these frameworks.

10:00

Introduce the first round with the following instructions.

The 1st Round of the "Battle"

↱ **Clearly state the objective: sharing knowledge.**

Comment: Have you seen movies where pilots (suspiciously looking like Spencer Tracy, Arthur Kennedy, or Tom Cruise) were briefed before going on a mission? The squadron commander and his intelligence officer stood in the front wearing cool pilots' gear, and spent a few hours intensely briefing the crowd. Maps, routes, and intelligence were communicated, and the pilots asked penetrating questions, until all knew exactly what to expect as they flew over enemy territory.

The first round is the equivalence of that scene, sans Tom.

↱ **Assign questions** to be answered by the competitor teams. (See Chapter 3 for the rationale behind these questions.)

1. Is your company happy with its current market position?
2. What are its hot buttons?
3. What are its blind spots?
4. ***The main task:*** *Based on your answers to 1–3, please make specific predictions about your company's likely reaction to the host's plan of reviving its brand.*

↱ **Assign the question to the host team.** The host team's task is to focus on question 3: Identify as many potential blind spots in the plan as the Blind Spots Analysis suggests. (See Chapter 3 for how to perform the Blind Spots Analysis.) The underlying question to answer: Is the current plan taking advantage of emerging opportunities and defending against emerging risks as the competitive landscape is changing, or is it wedded to obsolete assumptions and the old "conventional wisdom"?

↱ **Set the rules of engagement.**

- **Rule # 1:** Use intelligence to get in character. Do *not* make up assumptions about the competitor!
- **Rule # 2:** Predict what makes sense to the competitor (see "commitment to the circumstances" in Chapter 4), not what makes sense to *you*.
- **Rule # 3:** Listen carefully and take notes of the other teams' predictions. You'll need them for Round 2!

Comment: Reminding your participants to make good use of the intelligence briefing is a defensive move against the tendency to use unsubstantiated rumors, industry gossip, and personal beliefs to make predictions that are mostly intuitive, and mostly wrong. It is also a good rule to sidestep old internal corporate battles.

Highly recommended: Encourage participants, especially those on the host team, to be honest and to identify the "elephants in the room." Explain that, if they don't, competitors will, with much harsher consequences to the company.

↱ **Send them to do the analysis.**

Comment: Depending on time management in a game, which in turn depends on how many competitors are role played, a typical breakout lasts between one and a half and two hours.

1:00–3:00

Let teams present their findings.

Comment: Time management is crucial in an intense and information-packed day such as this. Whatever time is allocated per team, enforce it. Ask the teams to focus on essence, not details, and characters, not hypothetical conjectures.

Highly recommended: During these presentations allow clarifying questions but no debates. The reason is that the goal of the first round is to share knowledge, and each team has spent time "becoming the competitor." The last thing you want is someone's own biased opinions based on his experience with the competitor 15 years back to derail the intelligence delivered by a team playing the character of the competitor.

Snippets From the Snack Game

Excerpts from the LX Team predictions (market leader):

"The character of this dominant competitor is a *focused bull*. LX is focused on one line of products. It is focused on a clear business model: Global consumers are similar to each other in that they will buy LX products without a need for substantial customization for local preferences. LX is focused on R&D. Its strategic decisions are influenced by technology, *not consumer preferences*.

With its monolith global strategy and narrow product line, LX is 900 pounds of muscle: It has huge economies of scale and a far superior cost position to WP.

LX's possible blinder is its legacy: a core of historically significant products carrying older technology, appealing to kids but not to adults. They generate significant free cash flow so LX is reluctant to cannibalize them. Consumers are turning away from these products.

Is a bull ever in a relaxed mood? LX management is watchful over rising cost, and it seeks defense against global conglomerates moving into its territory with broad portfolios and higher market power over distribution channels. *A bull has to keep a close watch over his herd of female cows*. As a defensive maneuver, LX attempted a large diversification move itself, but failed."

Playing the character, the LX team made several predictions. Among them:

1. LX will not yield market share to WP even at a cost. Market share dominated LX's financial modeling (the influence of a particular large consulting firm enabled an easy prediction of what financial models dominated management thinking). In response to any attempt by WP to take market share, LX would use cash from its older core products to finance the fight. It would react aggressively, *like a bull*, using pricing actions locally wherever WP threatens its leadership. However, it would not initiate a *global* price war. This was *out of character. Bulls focus.*
2. Relentless in its cost-cutting drives, LX would pare down its product portfolio to globally significant brands. That would fit with large clubs' and discount retailers' drive to pare down the number of products they carried, and would hamper WP's plan of attack.
3. Having completed a methodical upgrading of its existing line, the bull will focus almost exclusively on getting the next breakthrough products. With WP aggressively going after its market share, it would speed up the BIG innovation.
4. *Bulls may be short-sighted and colorblind, but they don't give up.* LX will continue to seek acquisitions to diversify its line. The motivation is to counter the threat of large conglomerates yielding better bargaining position with large retailers.

In response to a question, the team made a specific prediction about China: "LX has been one of the first companies to go into China. It has a large new manufacturing facility there and a huge distribution network. It is very proud of its Chinese investment. It would respond strongly to an attempt to enter the market on a large scale. *It would be a red cape waved in front of a bull.*"

Team LX then rested.

The RR and the D teams make predictions:

Two additional presentations followed: RR, a European competitor with a strong base in Europe and parts of Asia and a smaller share in the United States, and D, an American company, very strong in a related industry but struggling in the market under war gaming. Both companies were privately owned, and quite secretive. Not much intelligence was available on them, but the character of each was relatively easy to discern with role-playing techniques. Companies with strong personalities are easier to war game and require little direct intelligence.

The teams portrayed companies that were more proud than well-managed, historically strong brands but stuck in old traditions. The character of both was closer to an *Old Nobleman* than an aggressive entrepreneur. If these companies were not private, they most likely would have been targets of an acquisition drive by one of the giant food and beverage conglomerates. The owners, though, showed no interest in being acquired. The question on everyone's mind was: Could they survive on their own? What was the future of profitable but smaller players in a market where the buyers—large distribution channels—continually consolidated? The teams predicted: As long as route-to-market included multiple smaller independent distribution points, RR would do nicely, despite its lack of clout with the large retailers. D, on the other hand, might choose to get out of the category altogether if its share kept shrinking. The team did not see D going aggressively after an acquisition in this beverage category. Because WP's plan targeted LX, both RR's and D's likely moves would be to improve features of their products and add incremental expansion of distribution, but stick to their roots and strongholds. *Old Noblemen do not renovate as long as the castle's roof is not leaking*. And when it is leaking, they sometimes just give it away to the public....

Team WP, the host team, presented the blind spots in the plan:

WP was once a market leader, but it has fallen to second and, in some areas, third place (as measured by revenues). Its corporate parent was a very large diversified conglomerate with a collection of mature businesses, and an overall tepid return on investment. Wall Street had not been very excited about WP, seeing problems in its future growth. WP has been missing out on many emerging markets, and has been beaten quite badly by LX in the United States.

The host team played no favorites in putting the elephants on the table. It labeled WP product line "tired" and went as far as suggesting that consistent quality had not been achieved. Quality problems in the past had caused some experts to view WP as a "has been" in the technological race in the category, they said. Lacking a quality edge, management had often resorted to price cuts to defend market share or gain entry. The problem was WP's cost structure, which was inferior to LX. So WP management had been propelled into a perennial cost-cutting mode, with little to show for it. The reason for the inferior cost position was WP's underlying business model: WP believed in offering products suited to local preferences. Its production had therefore been localized and fragmented. But even that business model was not always well executed: Though the motto had been "local globalization," in reality the products relied little on insights from local markets.

WP's plants and equipment suffered from years of low investment, a result of corporate neglect. R&D has been mediocre at best, the team pointed out, and looking for big, market-changing innovation was coming up short.

In distribution, a critical "success factor" in this industry, in several markets WP trailed LX in understanding retailers' needs and fighting smartly for premium shelf space.

The character the team role-played was that of a *tired, somewhat down on its luck, discouraged salesman* who no longer truly believed it could beat the larger competitor. In a fight against a bull, a frazzled matador could only hope for a miracle, which is how the team labeled the brand revival plan. It pointed out the plan was all about "stabilizing" the market, which, in essence, meant hoping it would not get any *worse*. The brand's plan asked for increased investment from corporate that would be used to go aggressively after LX, so it was clear it was based on more *money*, not a new *strategy*. How would the tired matador improve its position against the charging bull? Beyond generalizations such as "improve distribution," "lower cost," or "better understand the market," the brand revival plan was low on fresh thinking: "more of the same," as the team mercilessly described it, "with just more money."

As team WP put it in conclusion: "What are we doing? Are we trying to be LX only with less focus and *higher* cost?"

The room was very quiet.

■■■

3:00–4:00

Introduce the second round with the following instructions.

The Second Round of the "Battle"

↱ **State the objective:** to find ways to improve the host's brand revival plan.

Comment: At this point all teams revert to playing (and helping) their company. There is little value in playing a version of war games, popular with software-based simulations, whereby teams think about ways to improve on *competitors'* plans. Let competitors hold their own games. Hopefully, they won't.

Highly recommended: Disperse the host team among the other teams. The host team finished its main task: placing elephants in the room on the table. Its members, joining the analysis of the other teams, will bring their perspective on blinders to those discussions.

↱ **Assign the question** to be answered by each and every team: *How can we improve on the brand's plan in ways that will "proof" it to LX's, RR's, and D's expected moves?*

Comment: This seemingly innocuous question requires the teams to maximize the use of intelligence and analysis presented to them, and take into account the capabilities, motivation, and blind spots of the competitor they role played in the first round, as well as the limitations on their own company's potential moves. Outsmarting expected moves and responses requires more than creativity. It requires a reality check.

Highly recommended: You may elect at this point to introduce some tests of strategy such as internal, external, and dynamic consistency to help the teams think through their proposals. (See below.)

↱ **Set the rules of engagement.**

- **Rule # 1:** Evaluate the proposals for improvement presented by each team based on some predetermined criteria:

  1. **Internal consistency.** Do the proposals fit with WP's overall strategy available resources and skills? If not, what would be needed to close the gap? Do the proposals address WP's blind spots and how to overcome them?

2. **External consistency.** How do the proposals fit with the industry's evolutionary path identified in the first round?
3. **Dynamic consistency.** Do the proposals take into account LX's, RR's, and D's likely moves?

- **Rule # 2:** In attacking the proposed strategies, stay in character of the company you role-played in the previous round.

Comment: This round is intense, as teams attack the proposals, and teams defend their proposals "on the fly." Focusing on staying in character takes the "personal" aspect of the critique out of the equation.

Highly recommended: A bit of fun can go a long way towards diffusing, what may be a tense confrontation between a presenting team and the teams playing its opponents. Equip each table with Nerf balls (soft, spongy, colorful balls), which participants can then use to throw at each other without causing any injury. Advise the room that the balls are to be used only when a team's defense of a proposal does not meet the objections raised in the room, or replies are judged blind, arrogant, misinformed, or mostly empty cattle manure.

4:00–7:00

Let the teams present their recommendations and battle each other.

Comment: This round of presentations in actuality covers two or more rounds of market battle. Recall from Chapter 3 that research is clear on the inability of most of us to think beyond two or three steps ahead. In this round, a team proposes a strategy to overcome competitors' likely responses. The room reacts to this proposal with possible, in-character reactions from the competitors, representing a second round of responses. The team then defends its proposal, offering modifications if needed, representing a third round of moves. Unlike hypothetical computer-based war games, this is where realistic games should stop.

Modifications Proposed for Reviving the Brand

The three teams made a total of 18 proposals. Many did not survive the attacks, but the few that did revealed the following conclusions of this war game.

The Main Modification to the Brand Team's Plan

WP must do things differently than LX. This may seem obvious, but actually this was a major departure from the existing plan and past moves.

Supported by Specific Themes:

1. WP was not ready to attack LX directly and would not meet its corporate expectations if it tried. Instead, it should specifically target RR and D and take market share from them wherever possible.
2. WP should focus on large institutional distributors, where its parent already had strong relationship, and use its parent company's entire portfolio to help market penetration by its products. This was a departure from the random expansion of distribution on all fronts. It also limited the battle with RR, which was strong among small distributors.
3. Although WP would always have higher cost than LX, it must close the growing differential if it wanted to survive. Therefore....
4. In the short term to mid-term (two–three years), strategy must focus on retrenching and reorganizing with the aim of gaining production and distribution efficiencies.

5. Instead of attacking LX aggressively, the funds should be spent on revamping R&D. In the short run, R&D should focus on incremental improvements. In the long run it should focus on specific growth areas where LX was *not yet playing*.
6. WP's short-term marketing should focus on revitalizing its tired line: adding new features, reviving old marketing themes, and changing packaging. Advertising should focus on WP's strength in providing local answers to local preferences, a theme it did not emphasize before.
7. In the long run, WP should accelerate the market move toward a specific product-line/technology where LX was relatively weak.

Each of these strategic moves came with tactical activities and specific action agendas, such as approaching U.S. mass merchandiser's clubs with the goal of getting D's drink products replaced with WP's.

There was a lot of work ahead.

Proposals That Did Not Survive

Several options did not survive the battle. In response to an attack by the LX team, the idea of going into China was nixed (playing in-character LX, its team argued strongly against this move, calling it "a hot button with a billion tons dynamite behind it"). Instead, another proposed option that was later adopted was going into several other developing markets where LX was relatively weak, but RR was stronger (Eastern Europe and certain areas in South Asia). The probability of taking share from RR was deemed much higher. RR's objections were answered by a modification that called for the deployment of WP's parent company good relationships with mass distributors in those markets to gain entry. As a further refinement, the team proposed using a particularly popular product (from the parent company's portfolio) that was already a market leader in those developing markets as a lead-in. RR, which did not have a competing product, had to admit the proposal was both externally and dynamically consistent. But was it also internally consistent with WP's parent company's strategy?

One of the most interesting moments in the game came right then when a senior participant from another business unit admitted the coordination between her unit and the war gaming drink unit had been less than stellar. However, she supported the proposed strategy of re-thinking the approach to distribution in those developing Eastern European markets based on a *total portfolio*. When pressed on the "what's in it for you" issue (coupled with a salvo of Nerf balls from the audience accustomed to empty slogans of "total portfolio"), the executive made a surprise assertion that it was actually the drink product that may be an ace card with distributors in those markets, as it presented higher growth potential than her more mature line. She proposed a joint task force to develop the total portfolio propositions further in those markets.

7:00

Bring the game to a close with a clear conclusion.

Comment: Summing up a game in a productive way is crucial. Just thanking everyone is not productive (though it is polite). Participants have spent a very intensive, very hard day thinking, role-playing, confronting real issues and lifting heavy elephants. At this point you need to line up the strongest recommendations, arrange them in coherent and consistent themes, and assign follow-up tasks to translate them into action plans and budget spreadsheets. If further approval is needed before moving onward, inform the group on dates and your time line.

Highly recommended: Capture the analysis from the game. If participants used paper charts, assign someone to collect those and transfer them to electronic format. If participants used portable memory devices, make sure all presentations are available on one computer. Take care to safeguard the data. If the game was held off-site, make sure paper trails and documents are collected and shredded.

An Epilogue

Four years later, WP has emerged from its retrenchment with flying colors. Rising market share, aggressive entry into several developing markets, revitalized products, a revamped production and distribution organizations were clearly applauded by the popular business press, including *Fortune* and *Business Week*. Interestingly, LX was doing well also. All the market share gains came from RR and D. D selected to sell off several of its brands, confirming its team's predictions. The predictions of the team role-playing LX proved robust: Its drive to diversify was right on, as it acquired a large brand and a company in Latin America, both in related fields, close to its technology core. LX also came out with a big innovation; it was still a formidable competitor, but analysts were unanimous in declaring that WP was *a worthy opponent*.

There was a lot of work and terrific leadership behind WP's revival. The war game was just one small step in this transformation. But war games are the perfect tool to point the way forward.

Game 2: Launching a New Product

The Settings

The industry in this real-world game was pharmaceutical, an industry that considers itself a special case, with its own unique business model. Pharmaceutical managers will explain to you that their business is "exempt" from the rules of strategy learned in business schools. As the following war game demonstrates, it is not. I will expand on the game's background in order to allow the reader to follow it. If the industry becomes too convoluted for your taste, just skip to the next section.

The host was a biotech company about to launch a new drug, to be followed by two new molecules later on, all in the same disease area (dermatology). Let's call this new drug RFH (short for Relief from Hell). This was exactly what it offered the patients.

The new drug was entering a crowded market, which was getting more crowded by the minute. The agreed protocol of treatment among physicians treating this disease—the so called "gold standard" in treatment—was a bunch of old and inexpensive drugs. They were effective in the short term but had severe side effects, so their safety profile, as it was known in this industry, was not stellar.

As the host company's new drug was entering the market, two competing new drugs were right on its heels: They were due in less than a year, and maybe as little as four months, past its launch date. Together, this new class of drugs worked on a different mechanism than the inexpensive oldies. They had a different safety record, with less-severe side effects in the short term. (No one knew the long-term effect(s) yet.) They had a better efficacy (ability to treat the disease symptoms), but not for every patient. Among themselves, though, these new class drugs differed on safety and efficacy, but without a clear-cut winner (that is, none was superior to the other on both criteria). The host's drug seemed safer than but not as effective as the other two.

However, there were also two new class drugs used in a *different* disease that doctors prescribed as treatment for *this* disease. This practice is known as "off-label" use. One drug was moving out of the "off-label" status, as its manufacturer petitioned the regulatory agency for approval in this disease area as well. That drug and its parent company ("TH" in this game) were deemed the most threatening to the success of the host's launch. The other, also with good record in the different disease, showed no signs of going for on-label approval. Off-label use of drugs has been popular among physicians.

As noted: A crowded market.

More on the Disease Area

Patients suffering from the disease could turn to alternative treatment methods using non-drug therapies. The severity of the symptoms determined which treatments doctors selected. Further, certain patients could not tolerate the new class of drugs at all; others could not tolerate the old drugs. Some reacted well to substitute treatments; some did not.

And then there was this important issue: The new class of drugs was *much* more expensive, and the delivery mechanism much less patient-friendly than the old treatments or the substitutes.

Sound confusing? Imagine being a doctor. Most of the physicians' work has been guesswork: Try this, and let's see how you do. No good? Let's go to the next on the list. Blood test comes back bad? Let's stop this and try that. And so on. In the future, genomics (the science that can match patients with specific drugs based on their genetic makeup) might provide clues as to who should take what and expect what results, but genomics has not yet progressed that far.

The Plan to Be War Gamed

The VP in charge of the therapeutic area (TA, the pharma industry's equivalent of a business unit)[1] for which the drug was developed asked the brand team to prepare a launching plan. The team of six worked for eight months on the clinical and marketing message and the war game was ran when the results of the clinical trails were largely known, though not yet approved by the FDA. Sans unexpected objection from the FDA, approval was imminent.

Corporate expected the new class of drugs to be a major source of growth for the company. The company's lion's share of revenue and profits came from another TA, which was its founding area of expertise and still provided 90 percent of its cash flow. However, that area was no longer a star in terms of growth.

Against these expectations, the brand team put together a solid launch plan. However, a word of caution is due here, so you get a feel for the task at hand.

A solid plan does not mean a smart one. It means the plan was a typical "off the shelf" blueprint in this industry. Change the name of the drug, and the plan would have been adopted easily by another pharmaceutical firm, as they all did things similarly. This is known as "competitive convergence." Few industries have reached a state of as much competitive convergence as pharma. The reluctance to initiate a different way of doing things has some solid historical roots. For one, pharma top executives have been regulated to death and have had the good fortune that even their most mediocre products made them tons of money. Most pharma executives have been home-grown in this insular industry, with little perspective on any other industry. The basic pharma model itself has not changed: Large companies just spend more chasing few key opinion leaders (KOLs), throw salespeople in the thousands at more and more reluctant physicians, and hope for the best. The potential downside is so big—companies have been known to go under or be taken over once *one* promising product launch failed—that no one takes any risks being innovative. As a result, new launch plans are just copycats of each other. No one can blame a product manager who does what is conventional wisdom.

So the launch plan was solid but it did not stand a chance.

The Game's Structure

Team	Description	Products	Comment
J (host)	Biotech	New class	First to market?
OD	Various manufacturers	Old, inexpensive "gold standard" treatments	Existing products
A	Large diversified healthcare company	New class	Would launch shortly after J
B	Large Biotech	New class	Expected to launch a year later
P	Large Pharma	Off label	Existing product in another disease area
TH	Largest Pharma in this game; considered the biggest threat.	Off label	Existing leading product in another disease area

Hour-by-Hour Instructions With Commentary

Because we went through the mechanics of a game earlier in the chapter, let's jump directly into the dynamics of the game.

8:00

Here are the essential assumptions behind the brand team's intended launch plan, the way they were presented by the brand manager:

- We are the first to market with RFH.
- We are the first in our market to claim long-term control of the symptoms (with long-term use of the medication). Other medications can only claim intermittent control.
- We will claim RFH is "the most effective and safe." The off-label drugs may be effective, but they raise safety questions. (They were not tested specifically in this disease area.)
- We pledge to be the best company to deal with for physicians and patients.
- We are expensive, but we will mobilize patient groups to press insurers and government to approve reimbursement.
- The launch will use funding from corporate to recruit KOLs, and hire additional salespeople to reach every physician who treats patients in need of this medication.

Comment: There were very few surprises in this plan. It was an industry-standard blueprint.

10:00–12:00

Teams were sent to breakout rooms.

The questions they were asked to answer were focused on this disease area:

1. Is the company happy with its market position *in this disease area*?
2. What are its hot buttons in *this disease area*?

3. What are its blind spots regarding market developments *in this disease area*?
4. ***The main task:*** *Based on the answers to 1–3 above, what is your prediction of your company's likely response to J's launch of RFH? If you play existing products, how would your company pre-position RFH? If you play upcoming products, how would the launch affect your launch?*

Comments: These were the same questions as those in the previous game in this chapter, but with a focus on the specific responses to the launch. Because the medications for this disease area were part of companies' larger drug portfolios, and because companies play in various therapeutic areas (cardio-vascular, oncology, central nervous system, infectious diseases, dermatology), broader considerations would play a role, too. To keep the war game focused, though, make sure teams understand that these broader influences should be analyzed only as far as their influence *on this specific launch*. Thus, if a company regarded the disease area, or the whole TA, as marginal to its core business, this was an important predictor as to how its relevant TA will respond to RFH's launch.

It is also important to note that in the pharma industry a lot of information is public, and launch plans are not very secretive. Competitors knew company J, the host, was coming out with RFH. From mandatory filing with regulatory agencies, from scientific publications, and from competitive intelligence among clinical developers, competitors knew the compound's general characteristics and the results from early-stage clinical trials; they also knew some of the safety or efficacy issues. As a result, competitors often "pre-positioned" new compounds with physicians: Their salespeople visiting the doctors played down the upcoming product's importance, spread inaccurate information (always competitors, never the host!), and so on. This is the equivalent of salespeople knocking aside competitors' point-of-sale displays at retailers, so don't make a face please.

1:00–3:00

The teams presented.

For brevity's sake, here are their most notable characterizations of the competitor and the essence of their predictions.

Team OD's message:

The manufacturers of the old products were like *faithful and reliable mules*: They focused on production quality, not on innovation. They managed low-cost/low-margin business. They did not know how to use fancy marketing or bother with strong reactions to the new class: "You go guys with your expensive new class of drugs. We have no intention of spending marketing dollars against you. We have a solid if unspectacular business, which is marginal to our huge parent companies. On the other hand, our drugs *work*."

Audience: Define work!

Team OD: Until you prove otherwise, we are the gold standard; we do the job for most people. We do not *need* to define work; physicians know us.

Audience: Do you mean to claim you work in all cases?

Team OD: No. We help mostly the mild symptoms. But we don't need to work in all patients. Our strategy would be to pressure governments to impose "must fail gold standard treatment" first and our market would then be guaranteed.

Team A's prediction (new drug class, launch on heel of J's):

Company A was *a businessman among scientists*. "Our upcoming drug, which is in Phase III trials, will be best in class. It has a potential to become a blockbuster. We will start our pre-launch campaign shortly, using this message. Part of our strategy was capturing a large number of patients in the late-phase trial, and those are likely to stay with us."

Audience: Will you fight on price?

Team A: We have price flexibility. We price at premium where we can and at a lower price where we can't. Look at our record: Last year we discounted our X compound (used in another disease area) by 20 percent.

Audience (truly baffled):
How can you *afford* lower prices?

Team A: We are a diversified healthcare company, and we don't depend that much on high-margin drugs. Our company's earnings are growing at double digits, and the market is giving us a high PE ratio, higher than the industry average, probably because of our better diversification. Also, there is a consensus in the market that our strength is managing lower-margin business, something you spoiled pharma brats have no idea how to do. So even with lower prices, we will make more money than you!

Team B's message (new drug class, about a year away?):
Company B was characterized as *the wizard*. "Team A may claim a superior product but product alone is not enough; we are the superior marketers in this therapeutic area, by all intelligence accounts. When it comes to hype, KOLs' loyalty, and patient support, we lead."

Audience: But your product is weaker than ours!

Team B: It does not matter one iota! We would integrate it into existing treatment, make it part of a combination therapy (using it with another, more familiar product). We do direct-to-consumer advertising, and can get the patients behind our message. We make the product more patient-friendly to administer than yours. We don't need a clinically proven superior product to gain market share.

Audience: What are your goals for this particular launch?

Team B: As a rule, we go for number-one position in market share, and worry less about profitability.

Team P's message (the leading product in this disease area based on *off-label* use and prescriptions by specialists who treat *another* disease):

The team characterized company P as *a giant lost in the forest*. "Our company is in upheaval. We have a new CEO, people are leaving, our focus is on a different TA all together, the off-label use is relatively new, but it is growing."

Audience: So why should we worry about you?

Team P: Don't mess with a confused giant. He may squash you as he flails around! We still are the leading company in your therapeutic area (with other products for other diseases). As a result, we have more contacts with specialists working in this field than anyone else. Our driving force is efficacy, efficacy, and efficacy. Our drug works. It has a proven record, which you do not, even if it is from another disease area. The physicians trust it. The physicians trust *us*. You will have to go through us first before they give your drug a try. We will nail you on efficacy and proven track record.

Team TH's message (off-label drug that is about to get approval from the regulatory body for use in this disease area; considered the biggest threat to J's launch):

The team characterized TH as *old-world pharma*. "We've played this game before. We are a large, well-established pharmaceutical company. Our drug had a good track record in the other disease area, with mostly mild side effects. It is also cost effective, and this a message we will use against you."

Audience: Why do you bother with approval for *on*-label use?

Team TH: We are playing by the book. Our drug is losing steam in the other disease area. It had a leading market share there, but it is declining (Company P is taking its place), so we are looking to expand it uses to capture additional revenues. This is very much in character for us. Extending the uses of products is how you play the game.

Audience: So this is basically a desperate maneuver?

Team TH: It's not so much desperate as it is how you play the pharma game *if you are big old pharma*. However, it is definitely a rearguard war. We are not a big player in your therapeutic area, and we have no great relationships with your specialists. We just play it by the book.

Comment: Playing down a competitive threat is as important as playing it up in a realistic war game. Team TH did a good job of that.

Team J (the host) in full play:

(Go back to the beginning of the game and refresh your memory on the launch plan. Team J was picking it apart assumption by assumption.)

"Are we truly the first to market? The off-label use is not really that *off*-label. Patients who suffer from the other disease often suffer from 'ours' too, and the off label medication works. Moreover, it has a track record, and we *don't*.

Is it wise to attack the off label medication on safety? We have a compound in development that works on the same path. Attacking the off label compounds now will be shooting our own foot three years down the road.

How serious is the assumption that patients affect reimbursement policies?" The team kept hammering. "How long would it take for that public pressure to manifest itself? What do you do in the meantime when your drug is so expensive?

Is the 'long-term care' strategy a winner? Since when do insurers go for this logic?

How different are we from A's drug? They make the same claims of 'most effective and safe.' Is safety even the issue with this new class of drugs? Our salespeople suggest, and we have some limited market research showing, that *physicians in our market look at efficacy* first and foremost.

What does it mean to be the 'best company' for patients and doctors? What's behind this slogan?"

The team summed up its Blind Spot Analysis, sticking the knife deeper at the carcass of the launch plan: "On efficacy, P and A will claim better results. On safety, TH has a much longer track record in actual use. So what is our *unique* position?"

In an unusually quiet room, team J answers its own question as follows:

"The only advantage, *if* it is even a real advantage, is that we have the first move, on label, *for a short while*."

3:00–4:30

Teams are sent to develop improvement to the launch plan. Is it even possible to salvage the plan?

Comments: It is completely possible for a war game to send the plan for a complete overhaul. It is also possible to send a message to management that the initiative is wrong and the plan should be cancelled. War games can save millions and hundred of millions on plans that are executed without a real chance of success. Pharmaceutical companies today fail to meet expectations on 60 percent of their new drugs; 95 percent of all new food products fail. Even GE lost $400 million on its subprime originator's acquisition. *It is much better to war game and "lose", than forge ahead and lose.*

4:30–7:00

Teams battle over strategic options for RFH.

The format should be familiar to you by now: As a team presented its proposals for improving RFH launch, the other teams attacked, staying in character of their competitor's likely response. This free format, bordering on chaos (but never reaching it) and using Nerf balls to release tension, produced a slew of creative ideas, ranging from the tactical to the strategic. Two major insights emerged quickly:

1. These were the cards J was handed: The product was not sufficiently differentiated; clinical indications alone would not drive it. The war game should have taken place a year and a half earlier, when the product development could have been influenced, maybe even stopped, prior to incurring a huge sunk cost. At this point, smart positioning was the only possible savior.

   Comment: You may think, "Duh!" But you'd be surprised how many brand managers and senior executives in famous, prestigious and once successful pharmaceutical companies had not internalized this simple reality, which the participants in that room had. Superior strategy is about different positioning, not about product features, not even product "superiority."

2. Smart marketing must create *switching cost* if the first move is to mean anything. Otherwise, first move advantage will be very transitory.

How do you create switching cost for both users (patients) and decision makers (physicians)?

The teams suggested a two-pronged strategy for the patients:

- First, it called for using emotional appeal, not clinical appeal, in the main marketing message. The teams presented several messages in that light, and advocated the use of several non-traditional media, including very moving video interviews with patients, whose lives were changed completely with the arrival of RFH. The theme emphasized changing the discourse with patient groups from dry clinical data to choosing *freedom* (from the disease).
- Second, the teams proposed making the administration of the product the most patient-friendly on the market, using delivery technology that would be unique to this drug. That effort required substantially speeding up the development of a delivery mechanism then in early stages of development. Funding was to come from using a contract sales force, which was cheaper, rather than hiring more salespeople to push RFH, as the original plan called for. That required corporate to get over issues of "pride in our identity."

Creating switching cost for the physicians would be more difficult. Physicians in this therapeutic area responded to efficacy data mostly. They respond to KOLs' endorsements. The original launch plan called for spending significant resources on gaining KOLs' endorsements. The first-round analysis produced a healthy skepticism regarding J's ability to compete for KOL against the much-larger B and P. Instead, one team made a pitch that received unexpected support from several MDs on the teams. The strategy would be to subtly but clearly harness the business rivalry between specialists working in this therapeutic area against the specialists competing with them in the treatment of this disease from another therapeutic area. The pitch would be both emotional and accurate: "We have the only drug specifically approved for your area of expertise."

Comment: The specialists treating this disease have seen their business taken away by different specialists treating the other disease (which often occurred **simultaneously**) with their off-label drugs. The loss of income has been substantial, including loss of revenues from office visits as well as physician and nurse time in administering the product. A medical practice is a business like any other; giving specialists additional income streams will be a welcome development for them.

The Elephant in the Room

The positioning came with literally dozens of activities that would have to be successfully executed *before* the launch. Idea-sharing between different regions involving routes to market through pharmacists and nurses and patients were adopted. However, throughout this very productive second round the big white elephant in the room stayed quietly on the side: *pricing*.

Comment: What do you do when participants would not touch a taboo with a 10 foot pole? You have two choices: assume they know better, or risk your neck and put it on the table. I can't tell you what to do; I can only tell you what I did.

Drug companies have pricing power that is the envy of every industry on earth except cocaine manufacturers. As long as generics are absent, insurers and buyers (hospitals, pharmaceutical benefit administration companies, HMOs), pay *more or less* whatever pharma asks. And for biological agents, generics are basically non-existent.

This picture-perfect scenario is changing, though. Governments are starting to play a significant role in setting prices, both as the largest buyers and as regulators. Governments can refuse to allow expensive new drugs on an approved list (called formularies) and insurers then have little incentive to reimburse patients for using them. In some markets (Asia, for example), the whole insurer-drug companies game is nonexistent, and patients pay out of pocket.

Given this varied landscape, one would expect pricing to be at least an issue for discussion. In this game it was not.

So I put it on the table in unequivocal terms. "Do you really think you can buck the trend of lower prices?" I asked. "And if insurers balk at reimbursement, what kind of competitive weapon did you give your loyal specialists?"

The table creaked, seemed about to collapse, but held. A heated debate ensued, resulting in two revolutionary ideas for company J. The most important was basic: J must create an economic case for the benefits of using the compound. Insurers may then have a business rationale to look at it: If they were persuaded that a management of the disease with a lifetime therapy of J's product could lower the lifetime reimbursement expenses for these patients, insurers might have an incentive to examine the new expensive drug. This revolutionary thinking was called pharmaeconomics. It was revolutionary—not for the world of economics, but to the world of pharmaceutical companies when this game was played. Some large pharma companies created pharmaeconomics departments to tease out economic rationale for treatments, but largely this new approach was used sparingly or not at all. Pharma was ruled by science and clinical data for the most part.

The other proposal adopted was to share the risk with the disease specialists. Provide them with three months of free-sample supplies so they could hand them to patients. Hopefully, by the end of the three months, the company would be successful using the pharmaeconomic case in getting the drug approved for reimbursement in *some* markets. Risk-sharing with doctors was not a new idea. It was only new to company J, where pricing had been considered a taboo, outside any debate, dictated from above (top management, not divine), and was to be accepted without questioning.

7:00

The exhausted VP of the TA thanked the participants. In summing up the game's recommendations, he did not attempt to "sugarcoat" the situation. It was clear that the improvements did not proof the plan against competitors P and B, or A, who had the resources to blunt J's launch. But it was also clear that without the improvements the launch was doomed. The new strategic positioning of RFH provided the brand manager with some reasonable differentiation, which strengthened its odds of success.

Epilogue

Relief from Hell was launched in 2002. It did not meet corporate expectations. That was an impossible job. However, as this book is written, the compound's sales have been enjoying double-digit growth for several consecutive years. In 2007, for example, the drug was growing at more than 50-percent annual rate. Not bad for a "me too" drug with a so-so clinical profile.

Incidentally, the large pharma company TH, which pre-game discussions pointed as the most dangerous threat to J due to size and leadership position in the other disease area, proved a much-less-substantive threat than pre-game expectations. The team role-playing TH, which predicted this eventuality, did not see the fruits of its great role-playing. Its members were by then dispersed all over the globe, as is the case with professionals in this industry. But their legacy lives on at J.

The Games: Schematically

A Schematic Flow of a Game Aimed at Testing a Plan

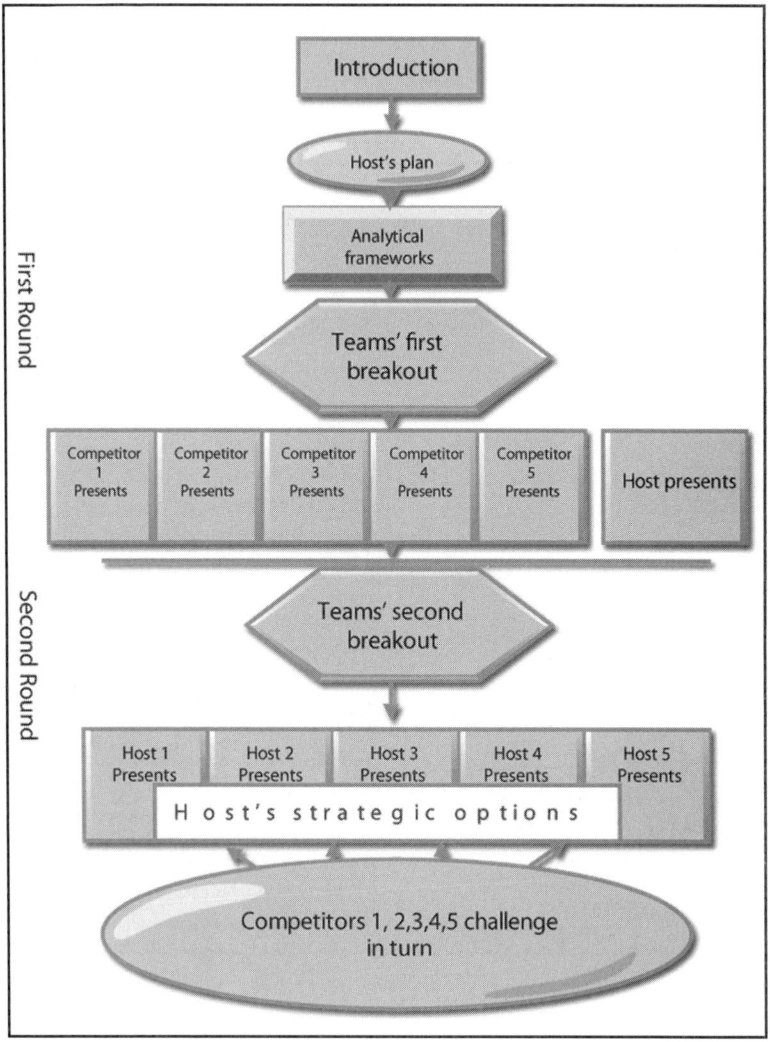

Testgame schematic.

Ending the War Game

The strategic options stage in a war game is a natural high for most participants. They get to express some serious creative strategic thinking, they get their butts kicked and kick some other butts in return, and the challenge is to harness that energy.

Here is a schematic flow of the ending stage of a war game:

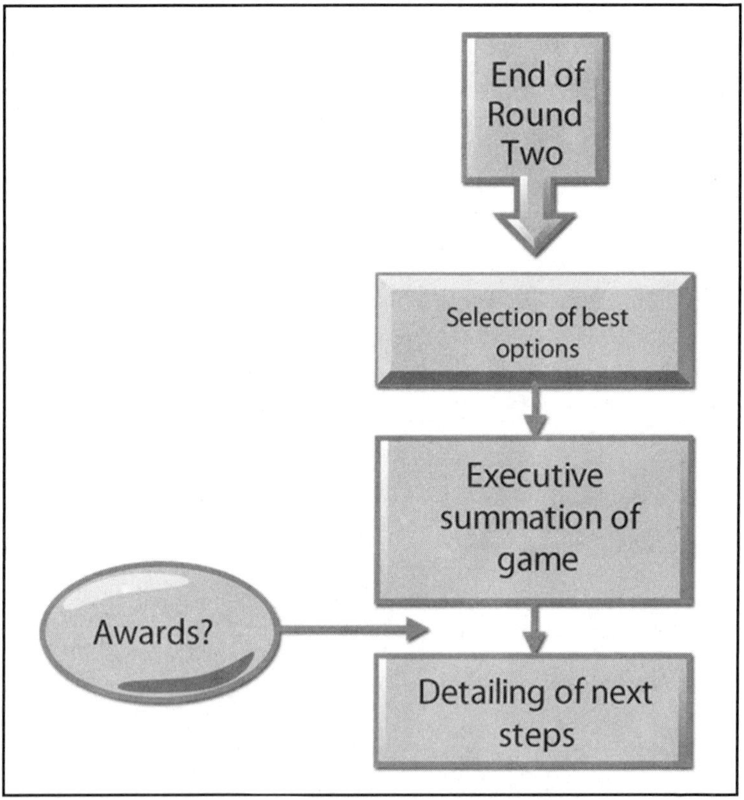

End game schematic.

This figure shows the right sequence at the end of a war game. The first step in ending a game is the selection of the most suitable and promising strategic options, among those passing the three strategic tests discussed earlier. There are several approaches to this step. One can use the participants themselves in a simple open voting session, to rank order options in terms of several additional criteria:

- **Uniqueness.** The potential of the strategic option to differentiate the company's position from the competition, and its source of competitive advantage.
- **Trade-Offs.** The ability of the company to defend this new position against competitive convergence. How fast and how easy would it be for competitors to imitate that strategy?
- **Change.** The distance of the option from the company's existing activity chain and how much of a change is this option from the company's existing capabilities and practices.
- **Time.** How long would it take to implement?
- **Price.** What's the cost?

Although you should exercise some caution not to put down the hard work done by the teams whose options are not selected, participants themselves tend to easily recognize superior options and harbor no hard feelings about those options which are rejected. In other words, they are not children, and there is no need for soft paddling.

Following the rank ordering of strategies, management may opt to grant some prizes. (A trip to Paris is always well received, though most don't realize there is such place as Paris, Texas!)

At that point in the game, the game sponsor must take charge of the room. He or she must sum up the new things (s)he learned, and the lessons (s)he takes away from the workshop.

The end of a game should also include a concrete outlining of the next steps. Remember that war games must be transparent, and that includes transparency as to the way management intends to use the game's outcomes. Significant good will can be gained with a few simple, common sense moves by the sponsoring manager. The next chapter takes you through some specific suggestions on implementing a game's recommendations.

Highly recommended: However you aim to end the game, and however you decide to structure its flow, never lose sight of what is important in running a war game:

1. It has to be Realistic—no computers or software.
2. It has to Empower you to walk away from a bad plan.
3. It has to be Accessible to all managers throughout the company.
4. It has to be Lots of fun to engage people's imagination.
5. It has to be Inexpensive—no army of consultants.
6. It has to be Simple—so you can run it yourself.
7. It has to be Transparent—no backroom algorithm or hidden agendas.

No computers, no software, no army of consultants—just good, old-fashioned role-playing of others' perspectives so yours has a chance of standing out, at a fraction of the cost of market failure.

Chapter 11

Implementing the Game's Results

Games are exciting, but then there is the day after. How should you manage the expectations of participants for action, based on the game's results? This question ties to a broader one: How does one assess the value of a war game? If management does not act on the game's recommendations, is the game a complete failure?

The answer is not a simplistic yes. Sometimes the value of a good war game manifests itself months later. It is important to understand the hidden benefits of war games—benefits I have seen in unexpected places. As war games become inexpensive and popular, I hope they reach down in the organization and serve many more goals than just the stated one of testing or formulating specific plans.

This chapter covers the obvious issues of how to use the intelligence analysis performed during the game to further the company's market knowledge, collection of follow-up information, identification of indicators and milestones for market and competitive events predicted by the war game teams, and so on. This chapter also covers the less-obvious mistakes management should avoid in post-game implementation, including unnecessary secrecy, communication blackouts, and the watering down of the game's results. Simple management gestures can magnify the benefits from a game several-fold.

Here are some steps you should take at the moment the game is over, after the formal "thank yous."

At the End of the Game...

Step 1: Collect All Analyses. If the teams used flip charts, collects the paper charts. It is naturally easier to record the analyses electronically, and then "collect" them into one summary file of the game. The reason you should collect the analyses is that within a week following the game, you should disseminate them (see Step 3).

Step 2: Do Not Leave Confidential Documents in the Room. War games touch on sensitive subjects and are often done off-site (though this is not necessary for small, intimate "family-only" games). Intelligence briefings should be collected and shredded. Let competitors find out how much you know about them through your market action, not through sloppy counter-intelligence measures.

Within a Few Days...

Step 3: Disseminate a Summary of the Game Among Participants. If you want people to help you again, make sure their efforts are appreciated. Many people who came to your war game did not have to be there. They would like to know that you paid attention to their work.

Before you send the final draft of the game's summary, ask each team's leader (or some other team representative) to go over your summary of their competitor analysis and their recommendations for plan improvement. That way you ensure that what is disseminated reflects their insights.

Implementing the Game's Results

An effective war game produces a list of improvements for the existing plan, or a list of options for a new plan. In either case, the team in charge of drafting and executing the plan is the one that should use these recommendations to strengthen its proposal, and it is the prerogative of that team's leader (the product director, the brand senior director, the area VP, and so forth) to decide which recommendations will be implemented and which will not. Corporations are not democracies, and, even if teams believed a particular action must be taken, it is completely possible that further deliberations resulted in a different course of action. So far this is obvious, and the vast majority of game's participants understand this dynamics. There are several steps management can take, though, to make sure the game's energy and the knowledge generated during the game are preserved for future benefit.

Communicating Decisions

Games are group efforts. The group as a whole deserves to know what has become of its effort. This is simple courtesy: Management should send an update to the game participants. It would be wise to explain why certain actions were chosen over others. In my decades of experience, I've never heard anyone complains about knowing too much. I *have* heard a lot of "If they did not want my input, why did they ask for it?"

I am often confounded by excuses of confidentiality and "need to know" used by management that elects not to share its deliberations and rationale. If the war game's participants had high enough clearance to take part in the game, they should be trusted enough to share in the thinking behind the decisions. It is also the best way to ensure alignment with the final plan and strategy. Paranoia is a good quality in prisons, not in corporations.

Reaping Hidden Benefits

War games create a "competitive database" that can last for years if stored and updated effectively. The interpretation of the basic intelligence, the character created, and the predictions made are what knowledge management experts call intellectual capital. To get a return on this capital, one needs to turn the competitor character built up in the game into an on going competitor *expertise*. These simple steps will ensure effective use of the capital:

- Store the predictions and the rationale behind them in a file.
- Ask someone from the competitor's team to follow up on the predictions within a certain time period, and update you.
- If the predictions were off, analyze the reason and update the competitor's character.
- If the predictions were on target, notify other members of your organization that you are more than willing to share this competitor's expertise with other teams as the need arises (such as their product launch or market penetration plans).
- Make sure to "cc" top management on the previous memo. It can't hurt, can it?

Strengthening Intelligence Capabilities

A war game uncovers your organization's intelligence capability—or lack thereof. You can ignore it, or you can capitalize on the findings.

- The game revealed major intelligence gaps: critical things you didn't have a clue about. Consider the ramifications and decide if it is time to push for dedicated intelligence resources inside the organization. Many organizations create a position of competitive intelligence manager following grassroots' demand from marketing and sales managers.
- The game revealed minor gaps: tactical details you would be happy to have had but actually affected no real change in your strategy. Don't rush to spend money on getting these details. The "good to know," insatiable demand for tactical information on competitor is a waste of resources. Keep your limited resources focused on major intelligence needs—those that help you understand the essence of the competitor's character, not his every little move.

Chapter 12

Strategic Junctures[1]

by Helen Ho and Matthew J. Morgan

You are now ready to prepare, organize, and run a game. This chapter provides you with some ammunition to convince your bosses, who may not read this book, that introducing war gaming into your company's decision-making process can be a bonus saver.

How do you prove a war game is effective? You can take my word for it, but naturally, because I run war games for a living, I'm a tainted source, and I assume you are smart enough to suspect that consultants hide their failures. (Anyone remember McKinsey's role in the collapse of Enron? The trouble at its clients, Global Crossing, Swissair, and Kmart?[2]). I don't expect you to just take my word for it. Instead, I'll provide you with hard evidence. The problem is that I can't use companies I worked with for confidentiality reasons.

So here's a solution: I'll demonstrate the effectiveness of war games using Hindsight Games. In Hindsight Games, I picked companies I *did not work with*, that made a major decision, and traced the effect a hypothetical war game could have had on changing the outcome of that decision. I realize this is tantamount to kibitzing after the fact (that is, interfering or giving unwanted advice), but this is kibitzing with a good purpose.

When Is Hindsight Valuable? Not Always

Hindsight is wonderful: You look back, and you see what you should have done differently. Yogi Berra is credited with saying it is hard to predict, especially the future. In contrast, people dismiss hindsight as *easy*. It is anything but.

For hindsight in strategy to have value, one must demonstrate that, *given the available information*, the decision could have been better. In other words, you can't fault a manager for taking action based on his experience, intuition, and common sense if the data available at the time were so ambiguous or so limited that, given the same circumstances, he would have done the same thing again. So hindsight lessons refer to situations where a manager ignored available data.

Hindsight Games are best understood in the context of *strategic junctures*. The best way to understand the concept of strategic junctures is to think of a junction in railroad tracks. A few seconds before the train gets to that junction, the driver must make a decision: "Do I go on the right track, or do I go on the left?" (In actuality, a central switch makes the decision for him, but the analogy stands.) In business context, the definition is as simple as the following statement:

"Looking back, we should have done something three years ago."

As nonacademic as this definition may sound, every manager knows this feeling at least once in his career. If a company does not take action at a strategic juncture, it is bound to wake up in a crisis. War games are perfect tools to use at strategic junctures. Used too early, they waste energy at the wrong place in the time line of industry evolution. Used too late, and they waste money on trying to change course for a train running at 100 m.p.h.

I will be the last to claim strategic junctures are easily discerned from white noise afflicting managers' attention. Author and organizational learning guru Peter Senge says that organizations are mostly equipped to react to big changes in their environment. The metaphor he uses is not original but it is effective: A frog placed in a pot of a cool water on the stove while the heat is slowly turned up would stay until it gets too disoriented from heat exhaustion to get out of the pot. Organizations face a similar risk. They may ignore strategic signals until it is too late. Accordingly, the case studies you are about to read have been selected based on these two criteria:

1. They show how companies can see nothing and hear nothing until they are hit on the head with a 2 × 4. The point we make is how a strategically placed war game could have saved the day...and a few million dollars.
2. They are based on publicly available information, which would have easily been introduced should a war game had been held at the strategic junctures. In other words, if a war game was to have been played at that critical point, *with the available public evidence*, chances are managers would have picked up on the market signals. Accordingly, we present the cases in chronological order, the way they unfolded at the time, with references provided to newspaper and news agencies reports. Management's lesson from these cases should be simple: If you *allow* the signals in, the market will tell you what's wrong.

The Fox That Outfoxed the Mouse

Watching sports on television is a beloved American pastime. And the television business is all about attracting eyeballs, thus delivering viewers to advertising messages. This is a story about one newcomer network, Fox, that in a very short time emerged as a key competitor to the undisputed market leader in sports broadcasting, Disney's ESPN. ESPN had completely dominated the sports channel market until Fox Sports blasted onto the scene, literally out of nowhere, in 1996. In

2006, Fox Sports was a close second in the U.S. market, boasting a reach of 81 million U.S. homes to ESPN's 89 million.[3]

The amazing story of Fox Sports is a story of Rupert Murdoch and John C. Malone. Murdoch and Malone's business interests intersected when Malone's Liberty Media, a major cable operator, wanted to break the control that ESPN, a content provider, yielded as a virtual monopoly.[4] For Malone, 1990 was a turning point: That year his company, TCI, was forced by ESPN to pay a huge rate increase to keep it from pulling its content from its cable stations.[5] Malone was not alone. Many cable operators regarded ESPN as an arrogant monopoly.[6] The pent-up demand for competition was there. All it needed was a competitor.

In stepped Murdoch. He wanted to build Fox into a national empire. Fox Sports was an important brick in the wall. In 1988, he hired David Hill, a broadcasting executive with a very strong record of producing popular sports content in Europe. He headed the BSkyB sports channel and created Sky Sports. In the late 1980s, Hill created "Sports," a satellite service, and Eurosport, a pan-European cable sports service similar to ESPN. In 1990, he headed the joint venture formed by Murdoch and Malone. According to *Fortune* Magazine, the joint venture negotiated between Fox and Liberty included $350 million in cash for Malone's Liberty. In this partnership, Malone offered his full or partial ownership of several unprofitable regional sports networks.[7] These included the Prime stations in Southern California, Nevada, and Hawaii. In 1988, ESPN rejected the idea of buying Prime Network to start a regional sports network. By 1990 Liberty Media reportedly owned a 60-percent stake in these stations. ESPN's President and CEO quit to take a job with Prime Ventures (owner of Prime Network). Fox Sports Net was on its way.

ESPN's strategy unwittingly played into the partnership hands. To Disney, owner of ESPN, ESPN was a desirable product to bundle with less-attractive channels. This was heavily criticized by cable executives. As one executive bluntly stated, Michael Eisner was "killing the golden goose."[8] This bundling tactic was a stop-gap that would not last. Predictably, the FCC got stricter on preventing big cable operators from selectively bundling and withdrawing their channels in different markets. This action leveled the playing ground and ensured that Fox Sports content was available in every major market in the United States. This action could have been predicted looking at the history of FCC rulings on monopolistic bundling in similar contested markets.

Strategic Juncture 1: *The first war game should have been run by Disney shortly after Malone and Murdoch announced their marriage, and ESPN's CEO defected to the competition. David Hill, Murdoch's point man, was already in the lead, and his past history of building sports networks out of scratch should have been studied in a briefing book. Most of Hill's strategies were in the open, so intelligence collection should not have been a problem. Murdoch's ambition for Fox, in which Fox Sports was an important element, and Malone's interest in breaking ESPN's monopoly were also quite clear, upon a cursory analysis. The market frustration with Disney's bundling could have only escaped the attention of a fat, complacent overconfident management.*

What type of game? At that juncture, with mounting signs that Murdoch was going after ESPN leadership, and mounting evidence that Disney's bundling strategy was running out of steam, Eisner or ESPN's new CEO (remember, the previous one just left for Malone's camp), should have run a Landscape game, formulating strategic options for Disney/ABC/ESPN. Alternatives to the bundling should have been considered. It would have been a wonderful idea to role-play a cable operator and feel the heat. Or maybe role-play a regional TV franchise and get a sense of building *local* franchises as an option. Disney actually tried its hand much later at a local strategy in Southern California around 1997, but that was too little, too late, and too clumsy. The

FCC slapped Disney's hand for anti-competitive tactics (attempting to block Fox Sports Net access to local TV stations), and it had to withdraw.[9]

Fox Gets Serious

ESPN was confident its specialty programming could not be duplicated, due to the extremely high cost of buying and licensing content for a national audience. ESPN was right in that the capital barrier to duplicating its national network would deter most serious opponents. Fox had to pay significant premiums in the few incidents where Fox won the bid for national content to unseat the incumbent broadcaster. Rather than go head-to-head with ESPN, Fox took a hybrid approach to building content and coverage. In the beginning, Fox paid a premium for some national content, including the NFL rights for 1994 to 1997. But in most other cases, as it acquired TV broadcasting stations serving the top markets, it also secured the rights to the home games for local teams. Licensing some limited instances of national content gave Fox Sports legitimacy as a sports broadcaster. But licensing mostly *local* content allowed Fox to grow its geographical coverage without financially extending itself. Observers noted that the emphasis on catering to regional tastes helped Fox attract more fans outside the core diehard group that is very passionate about big league professional sports. By concentrating on attracting die-hard fans, ESPN felt it was delivering a niche demographic to advertisers. Fox Sports, on the other hand, was more concerned about attracting a larger, more diverse audience.

In 1993, Fox Television outbid CBS for the right to broadcast NFL games for the next four years, as well as one Superbowl (1997). It outbid CBS by $200 million per year. The decision to enter the sports market with national NFL football content was deliberate. Rupert Murdoch made this declaration in a *Sports Illustrated* interview shortly after the deal for the NFL games closed, saying, "We're a network now. Like no other sport will do, the NFL will make us into a real network."[10] *Sports Illustrated* approved of the choice: "For Fox the NFL package means instant credibility."[11]

What did ESPN do? ESPN ran ads that alluded to the possibility that Fox Sports would not be able to recruit two well-loved CBS football commentators (Pat Summerall and John Madden).[12] After Fox won the rights for the NFL programming, Hill promptly hired CBS's most popular announcers, and most talented producers.

The fact that Fox only bought one year of Superbowl broadcasting, at the end of the negotiated four-year commitment, should have been recognized as an audience-building tactic. The first three years of NFL broadcasting build sports broadcasting brand recognition among television viewers. By the fourth year, they compounded their audience draw by spending three years luring dedicated NFL viewers to their stations, and then drawing in an even bigger audience for the Superbowl. Because this was a somewhat abnormal entry, with only one year of Superbowl, ESPN might have been tempted to view Fox as less than serious. This would play perfectly into Fox's strategy of gaining a foothold while minimizing the expense of its investment. If the competitor made this mistake, Fox could even avoid the threat of a harsh competitive response. This is the same principle that guided every successful guerilla strategy since the dawn of time.

Then by 1997, Fox made its next move: It purchased Rainbow Media. Rainbow was a cable company based in Long Island, New York.[13] It owned and operated Madison Square Garden in New York City, as well as two major league sports teams (the New York Knicks basketball team, as well as the New York Rangers hockey team). This cable company had the biggest network of television stations in New York City metro area, with the highest revenue per subscriber in the industry.[14] However, in 1997, its parent company (Cablevision) was under fire from investors to raise returns. Rainbow Media had incurred $1.1 billion in debt due to the purchase of Madison Square Garden and other business-related expenses.[15] This cable company was a prime target for a white knight investor. Rupert Murdoch and John Malone were happy to step up to the challenge. In June 1997, Fox/Liberty Networks acquired a 40-percent stake in Rainbow Media, outbidding ESPN.[16] (Fox/Liberty Networks paid $850 million; Disney/ESPN bid 800 million.[17]) Rainbow Media used the proceeds from this investment to pay off the debt. This stake gave Fox Sports Madison Square Garden and the associated sports teams that played there. Rainbow was offering a totally vertically integrated hold on one of the most important U.S. advertising markets.

Strategic Juncture 2: *At this point in 1997, Murdoch was showing his hand. He was going after regional franchises—both teams and TV stations. The Rainbow acquisition must have come as shock therapy to Disney/ESPN. There was method behind the madness. ESPN at this point should have come up with a strategy to block Fox Net's slow but methodical search for opportunities to increase national coverage through acquisitions in major markets. A war game should have been run with questions such as these: Where is the next most likely market Fox will target? Who are the players in that market? How can we disrupt Fox Sports Net next play? But ESPN's management was asleep at the helm. And Disney's management had a huge blindspot. Sometime in 1998, Michael Eisner commented on Fox Sports' aggressive acquisition spree, saying "We generally can't compete with Rupert on cost. He's a much bigger gambler than we are—and by the way, it's paid off for him. I'm more a sleep-at-night kind of executive."[18] Eisner was wrong: Murdoch was not gambling. Eisner and his execs simply did not see the signals. They were sleep-at-day kind of executives as well.*

In November 1997, Fox Sports still did not have a presence in the Detroit area. Detroit is a top-10 market, and the home base for the major automakers. Local car manufacturers spend a lot of money on sports-content-related advertising. The pressure to acquire a presence in this city was very high. In order to become a credible competitor to ESPN, Fox Sports needed to have stations in all the top-10 markets. It also needed to cultivate closer relationships with the major automakers. The area had a set of television stations named Pro-Am Sports System (PASS Sports). Fox approached PASS Sports to acquire it. The owner, the *Washington Post*, had initially refused to sell its PASS stations to Fox Sports. The opening for Fox was the fact that PASS did not own the local major league sports teams. Detroit-area sports content was up for open bidding, and Fox won. The *Washington Post* was left with no content for its PASS stations. It had to sell the stations to Fox Sports, at a bargain price.[19]

ESPN should have partnered with PASS to put up enough money to keep Fox Sports from buying the cable rights to the Stanley Cup–champion Detroit Red Wings and the NBA's Detroit Pistons. ESPN was so slow to move, it only started inquiring about the availability of the Pistons' content after Fox had outbid PASS.[20]

The rest of the story is well known. By 2002, ESPN was in freefall. It lost 14 percent in rating during 2001–2002 as Fox strengthened its hold on the NFL, and ESPN was left with secondary sports, a declining NBA broadcasting franchise and a very expensive arm race with Fox to keep its slight lead in audience.[21] Fox Sports gained 12 percent in ratings during the same period. Even with the slipping ratings George Bodenheimer, ESPN's president, was still in denial, claiming, "It's not all about ratings."[22] ABC/ESPN eventually outbid Fox for Monday Night Football, but it saw the audience decline from 25 to 16 million people. And Fox was closing in fast.

ESPN's Strategic Junctures

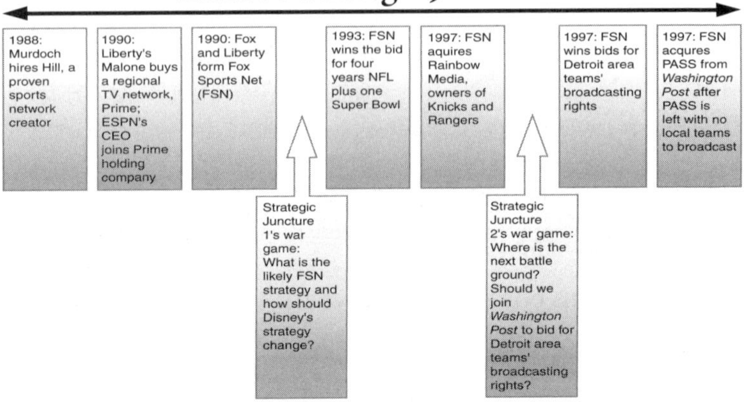

1988: Murdoch hires Hill, a proven sports network creator
1990: Liberty's Malone buys a regional TV network, Prime; ESPN's CEO joins Prime holding company
1990: Fox and Liberty form Fox Sports Net (FSN)
1993: FSN wins the bid for four years NFL plus one Super Bowl
1997: FSN aquires Rainbow Media, owners of Knicks and Rangers
1997: FSN wins bids for Detroit area teams' broadcasting rights
1997: FSN acqures PASS from *Washington Post* after PASS is left with no local teams to broadcast
Strategic Juncture 1's war game: What is the likely FSN strategy and how should Disney's strategy change?
Strategic Juncture 2's war game: Where is the next battle ground? Should we join *Washington Post* to bid for Detroit area teams' broadcasting rights?

Who Knew Flat Drinks Would Be All the Rage?[23]

Acquisitions present such a clear strategic juncture that one can only look in wonderment at executives, investment bankers, and high-priced law firms going at it without a shred of role-playing or attempt at gathering intelligence on other parties' most likely response following the deal.

In the Snapple commercials that ran on TV around 1993, Wendy Kaufmann (aka "The Snapple Lady") announced that Snapple was proud to be the third-runner-up in the drink market behind Coke and Pepsi. One would have to admit that the Snapple Lady was making some pretty audacious statements by putting the little drink-maker in the same league as two of the most venerable consumer brands in the world. But the growth potential of the new kid on the block was certainly noticed by Quaker Oats. In 1994, Quaker Oats showed Snapple that acquisition is the sincerest form of flattery. You may be wondering what would motivate a cereal company to buy a juice-flavored iced tea company. Quaker was simply trying to replicate the success it had experienced with its Gatorade acquisition. Quaker Oats bought Gatorade in 1983, and by 1993 this shining star was responsible for a whopping 25 percent of profits of the parent company.

The acquisition of a leading sports-drink brand (Gatorade) was a way for Quaker Oats to diversify its sources of revenue. In the early 1980s, Quaker Oats was a relatively small player in the ready-to-eat cereals market. Its biggest new hit in 1994, Quaker Toasted Oats, still only captured 1 percent of an estimated $8 billion cereal market. Gatorade was an excellent choice for entry into the sports drink market. At the time of acquisition in 1983, Gatorade controlled 86 percent of the market. Sixty other sports-drink-makers failed since 1983. There is little doubt that this bold move to diversify outside its core business gave the company a real boost. But it needed to do more. It needed to have more drink products in order to achieve the economies of scale and scope that the big cola-makers enjoyed.[24]

Quaker bought Snapple, outbidding Coca Cola, paying $1.7 billion. William Smithburg, Quaker's chairman and chief executive officer, explained the rationale behind purchase by saying, "Based on our success with Gatorade, we believe that Snapple has tremendous growth potential through increased penetration, broader distribution and international expansion."[25]

The purchase of Snapple in 1994 did not turn out to be such a good investment for Quaker Oats. It sold it at a big loss in 1997. What went wrong with Snapple, and what would a war game have done for Smithburg in 1994?

In the 1980s, at the time Quaker bought Gatorade, the Gatorade brand had largely flown under the radar of the big cola companies. The raging success that Snapple had experienced as an independent brand, which motivated Quaker Oats to acquire it in 1994, did not have such luck: It had caught the attention of the Coca-Cola and Pepsi *two years earlier*. Pepsi had teamed with Lipton to market Brisk, and Coke and Nestle joined forces to make Nestea Cool. Both major cola-makers had the advantage of having higher-margin products (the high natural juice content in Snapple squeezed margins), as well as larger distribution networks. Coke and Pepsi both enjoyed major advantages in economies of scale in both manufacturing and distribution. Snapple was a premium ready-to-drink tea and had marketed itself as a health drink. It was a drink that was more expensive to make and had a glass bottle. The glass bottle was such a significant expense that Coke's Fruitopia switched to plastic containers.[26]

Did Quaker pay enough attention to how it would compete with the giants? It was not obvious from its distribution strategy, where it was going up against the much larger cola producers. Quaker had effective distribution of Gatorade through a warehouse-delivery model. Gatorade was shipped from the warehouse directly to chain stores and other retail facilities that attracted a large number of consumers. Quaker Oats used its strong relationships (as a cereal manufacturer) with supermarket chains to negotiate prominent shelf space for Gatorade. Gatorade was a mainstream sports-oriented brand that appealed to both serious athletes as well as couch potatoes who admire athletes as role models. In the early 1980s, Gatorade had Michael Jordan, the legendary NBA basketball player, as its spokesperson.

In contrast, most of the distribution agreements Snapple negotiated were with smaller independent, mostly health food, stores. This model is known as DSD (direct store delivery). As rumors of Snapple being an acquisition target circulated, industry analysts expressed doubts about the match of Snapple with the warehouse distribution model. By moving into major supermarket chains, Quaker had to introduce the Snapple brand to the mainstream public. That was not as easy as Smithburg and his investment bankers thought. As Quaker/Snapple lost customers from its original base in the health food stores, it was unable to gain an equal or greater number of customers from the mainstream channels, where Coke and Pepsi had much more leverage. The change of distribution model resulted in a rapid loss of market share.

Is this just perfect hindsight? If it is, no war game would have helped. But this is not the case. A month before the acquisition was closed, Jean-Michel Valette, a beverage industry analyst with Hambrecht & Quist, commented on the rumors that Coke or Pepsi were considering buying Snapple: "I don't believe it; both Coke and Pepsi have entries into this category. They also have entirely different distribution systems, which would have to be integrated."[27] Having a mixed distribution model was not an option.

Quaker's CEO said, "We expect to create the most innovative distribution system in the beverage industry, combining the very best of the two organizations and enhancing value to our trade customers through more merchandising, more points-of-sale and more in-store refrigeration equipment."[28] In itself, no one can fault him for having this optimism. Perhaps Quaker would have been able to pull the hybrid distribution model off where even Pepsi and Coke could not. But for that, Quaker needed the support of Snapple management. Alas, Snapple was run by hippies. Gatorade was mainstream brand management. Any group of observers with no self-interest in the deal would have questioned Quaker's ability to integrate the two very different cultures.

Tom Pirko, president of Bevmark Inc., a New York–based consulting firm predicted at the time, "You'll have a lot of independents out there who are going to scream"[29] if Quaker tries to change that network. Quaker proposed an arrangement whereby it would sell both Gatorade and Snapple directly to the chains and the distributors would handle both products for the "mom and pop" segment of the market. Snapple distributors, who felt they deserved a share of the credit for establishing the brand, resisted the changes Quaker proposed. One of the distributors was quoted as stating that Quaker "just didn't know our business."[30]

Strategic Juncture: *Was Smithburg a visionary or overconfident? The difference may lie in attention to details. If Smithburg* *took part in a war game in 1994, prior to deciding on acquiring Snapple, the clash of Snapple's culture with his own Gatorade people would have surfaced quickly (assuming the Snapple team role-played accurately). Other options may have been more consistent with Gatorade's strategy, strengths, and character. The resistance of Snapple's distributors may have come to light if anyone had bothered to role-play Snapple as just one option. It is likely, though, as acquisitions go, that Snapple was interested in selling, investment bankers presented this as a great financial deal, and a phone call between the two CEOs sealed the deal.*

During the period Quaker controlled Snapple (between 1994 and 1997), Snapple lost 23 percent of its annual revenues. All of Coke's non-carbonated brands combined showed a sales volume increase of 50 percent for the period of 1996 to 1997.[31] In 1997, Pepsi reported that the Lipton Brisk brand experienced "double digit growth," and their Diet Pepsi and Mountain Dew brands experienced "single digit growth."[32] On March 1997, Quaker Oats sold Snapple to Triarc for $300 million. By the time of sale, Snapple revenues dropped from $689 million in 1994 to 550 million.[33]

The new owner did not do so badly: CEO Mike Weinstein led the volume of Snapple back to its 1996 levels for the second half of 1997.[34] In 2000, it sold Snapple to Cadbury Schweppes for $986 million. At $600 million profit in less than three years, we can only guess that Triarc executives war-gamed this acquisition quite well.

Interestingly, Triarc's CEO made a point of crediting this same disparaged DSD model for revitalizing sales at Snapple, saying, "The prior owner (Quaker's) marketing focus on selling Snapple through supermarkets had left the brand's traditional distribution network wondering about its role in Snapple's future. We convinced them of our renewed commitment to the sales model that made Snapple such a success in the first place."[35]

Quaker Oats' Strategic Juncture

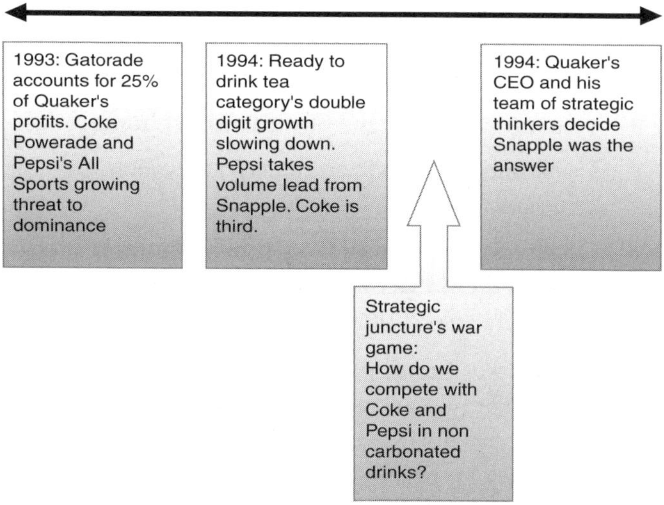

1993: Gatorade accounts for 25% of Quaker's profits. Coke Powerade and Pepsi's All Sports growing threat to dominance
1994: Ready to drink tea category's double digit growth slowing down. Pepsi takes volume lead from Snapple. Coke is third.
1994: Quaker's CEO and his team of strategic thinkers decide Snapple was the answer
Strategic juncture's war game: How do we compete with Coke and Pepsi in non carbonated drinks?

When Technology Culture Blinds the Decision-Makers

Technologically focused companies tend to miss out on social/demographic changes that greatly affect the buyer in their industry. A war game is one of the only measures that may—and I emphasize *may*—save such a company from an inevitable competitive disaster. Such war game may have saved Motorola (and Chris Galvin) from a technology "lockup" period, if only they ran one. Read on.

At one time, mobile phone usage was considered such a luxury that mobile handsets were status symbols. In 1987, Gordon Gekko (the character in the movie *Wall Street*) was featured in a key scene where he conducted business on a mobile car phone. In those early days of mobile telephony, Motorola was the leading manufacturer. As the mobile phone market expanded, evolved, and diversified, Motorola fell behind in market share against its rivals. What warning signs Motorola missed in the mobile handset market?

Looking back, these were key market changes that Motorola was ignoring:

- Mobile phone usage became democratic: The market exploded with rapid consumer adoption.
- Consumers favor small inexpensive phones.
- Consumers use style and design as selection criteria for phones.
- GSM (Global System for Mobile communication) became the de facto mobile device platform standard around the world.

Motorola was slow to recognize the consumer market potential for mobile telephony. It was selling phones that were more expensive than the competition at a time when the cell phone adoption rate was exploding. The rising number of cell phone users indicated that this type of product/service was becoming increasingly popular. Mass-market consumers were more cost-conscious than business users. In August 1990, Nynex (a predecessor company to Verizon Wireless) announced it was investing more than $100 million in a second cellular network on the East Coast.[36] Nynex explained that the intended purpose of this network was to serve pedestrian mobile phone users. Up until then, Nynex's first network was intended to primarily serve car phone users. During the same year the Bronx Borough in New York City adopted a new area code in anticipation of growing adoption of mobile phones and fax machines.[37]

Strategic Juncture 1: *At this point the shift from business to consumer adoption was in its early mode. That is the time a company can formulate a strategy to influence and lead the structural change rather than let the change lead it (into a crisis usually).*

In 1991, *The Economist* predicted the widespread adoption of mobile phones.[38] The cellular Telecommunications Industry Association corroborated this prediction. In March 1992, it reported that the number of American cellular phone subscribers grew more than 40 percent between 1990 and 1992.[39]

Back in 1990, just as Nynex was anticipating the widespread adoption of "pedestrian" mobile phones, the ballpark price for a handset was $1,000. At that time, analog phones were relatively big and bulky, and did not have many features that are now considered standard on even the most basic handset.

Prices of Phones Dropping

1990	Phones cost "more than $1,000 each."[40]
1991	Mobile phones were "well under $800."[41]
1992	Phones were on average about $400–500.[42]
1993	Car phones, which in 1991 went for $600, were now $200 or less. Pocket phones, which in 1991 cost $2,000 or more, cost as little as $200 when under certain service contracts.[43]
Present	Phones are far more advanced than those available in the early 1990s and are now available free under certain contract arrangements.

During the late 1980s, the technical standards organization (the IEEE), interested academic researchers, and the mobile telephony equipment manufacturers, were working together to decide which digital mobile telephony standards would be adopted. Europe decided to go with the GSM standard, which experts in the technical community predicted would become the pervasive world standard.[44] Even the first digital network in North America (built out by Rogers Cantel Mobile Communications) was a GSM network.[45] Motorola made the choice of backing standards that primarily had support in

North America (first TDMA, and then CDMA).[46] The migration to the GSM as the world's de facto digital mobile standard was an important early warning sign that Motorola missed.

Strategic Juncture 2: *It was time to make a technology bet. But technology is not a strategy. Even if the bet on technology was wrong (which one does not know until well into the future), the creation of a large and global mass market in cellular phones meant only one thing: Cheap competition from Asia was bound to emerge, as cost pressures mounted. That was the case for every bit of electronic appliance since the TV. Motorola's management should have developed and tested potential strategies against lower-cost producers. While at it, it could have asked itself if its product stylists ever visited Europe....*

Even back in 1990, Motorola derived 44 percent of its mobile phone sales from overseas markets. By 1995, the proportion of sales derived from overseas markets had risen to 64 percent. In 1996 *The Economist* reported that Motorola's internal forecasts projected that 75% of sales would be derived from overseas markets. Motorola anticipated that this expansion would be driven by customers in Eastern Europe and China buying cell phones to circumvent ailing local telephone networks. Despite the fact that Motorola was well aware of the fact that GSM handset sales would grow (as legacy analog technologies became obsolete), it chose not to act on this information.[47]

At Motorola in the 1990s, the mobile handsets and the mobile infrastructure groups were separate divisions run by two highly charismatic managers. In the early 1990s the manager of the wireless infrastructure division correctly forecasted the need for digital mobile handsets. However, the manager of the handset division was too focused on U.S. markets, which were slow to roll out the domestically adopted digital CDMA standard. The handset division manager "killed all prototyping projects for digital handsets."[48] When demand grew quickly in Europe, Motorola had nothing competitive to offer.

When Motorola missed the signs for the rapid adoption of cellular phones by consumers, it missed the early opportunity to adapt. Consumer market users are more fashion-conscious when they select their phones. The market had shifted to a paradigm where phones were sold using catchy marketing campaigns and esthetics became a selection factor. Nokia understood the importance of this market shift. For years it outdid Motorola on the stylishness of it phones. In 1999, Forbes reported that Nokia's chief designer, Frank Novo, was formerly of BMW.[49] Throughout the 1990s, Motorola was unable to introduce a phone design that gained popularity; its approach to design was too utilitarian.

Could Motorola have done better? It had two strategic junctures, each of them offering opportunities for a war game that could have changed Motorola's strategy. In retrospect, Ed Zander, Motorola's chief since 2004, did take those turns with the RAZR, Motorola's stylish and sophisticated handset. Chris Galvin could have done it years earlier if he trusted war gaming.

Motorola's Strategic Junctures

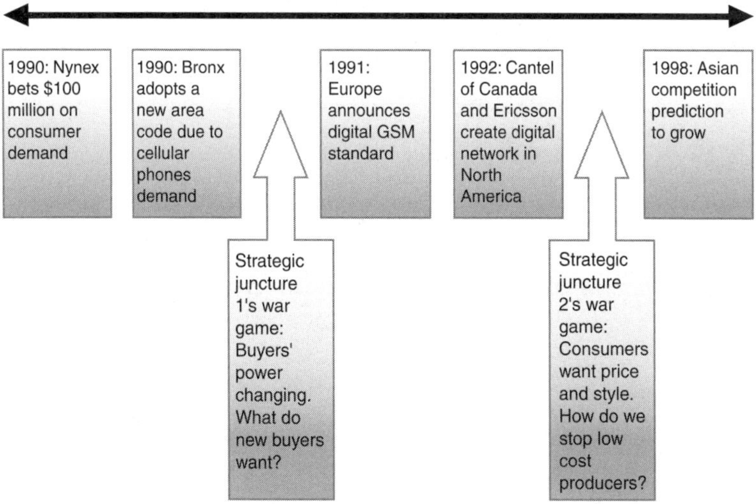

Chapter Notes

Chapter 1

1. Rosenzweig, *The Halo*, pp. 115–116.
2. Adler, *The Technique*, p.26. Among her students were Marlon Brando and Robert De Niro.
3. Bossidy and Charan, *Confronting Reality*, pp. 225–226.
4. Jones, "It's Lonely," p. 2B.
5. Tully, "In This."

Chapter 2

1. This chapter benefited greatly from heavy contributions by Michael Sperger, formerly of IBM and currently of SAP, and David Hartman of Strategic Surprise, Ltd. I added the sarcastic remarks and, of course, am responsible for any remaining errors.
2. Koch, *A History*, p. 160.
3. "Little Wars."
4. Ibid.
5. McGirt, "Getting," p. 94.
6. Ibid.

Chapter 3

1. Dana and Loewenstein, "A Psychological," pp. 252–255.

2. This is the area called Brodmann 10, and it is located in the prefrontal lobe. For more on these fascinating studies, see Camerer, Loewenstein, and Prelec, "Neuroeconomics."
3. Ibid., p. 21.
4. Kahneman, "A Perspective."
5. Camerer, Loewenstein, and Prelec, "Neuroeconomics," p. 29.
6. Carter, *Mapping*.
7. Camerer, Loewenstein, and Prelec, "Neuroeconomics," p. 38.
8. Ibid., p. 46.
9. Milicia, "Web."
10. Sidel, "Broader."
11. Weber, "J.P."

Chapter 4

1. Rotte, *Acting*, p.134.
2. "GE Chief," p. 1B.
3. Kissel, *Stella Adler*, p. 48.
4. Ibid.
5. Bossidy and Charan, *Confronting*.

Chapter 6

1. Jones, "It's Lonely."

Chapter 8

1. Porter, *Competitive*, p. 129.
2. Oster, *Modern*, p. 80.
3. Cubbin and Geroski, "The Convergence."

Chapter 9

1. Woodyard, "Car," p. 1B.

Chapter 10

1. A disease area might be, for example, lung cancer, and the TA it belongs to will be oncology. The intestinal disease colitis will belong to a TA for gastroenterology, which might also include drugs for other intestinal diseases.

Chapter 12

1. The research for this chapter was provided by Helen Ho and Matthew J. Morgan.
2. "Business."
3. Yahoo Finance. Accessed July 27, 2006.
4. Deutschman, "Sly," p. 68.
5. Davis, "Television's," p. A16.
6. Lowry, "ESPN's."
7. Fabrikant, "Broadcasters," p. D1.
8. Lowry, "ESPN's."
9. Turner, "Fox."
10. "Out Foxed," p. 16.
11. Ibid.
12. Hill, "Fans Wonder," p. C7.
13. "Fox/Liberty," p. 16.
14. Lesly, "Cablevision."
15. "Fox/Liberty," p. 16.
16. Sandomir, "Broadcast," p. D2.
17. Sandomir, "Cablevision Locks Up Garden," p. D5.
18. Rose. "There's No."
19. "State of Competition."
20. Sandomir, "Broadcast," p. D2.
21. Vranica, "NBC, ESPN."
22. Lowry, "ESPN's."

23. This segment is based on McGraw, Patrick, "Quaker Oats and Snapple," MBA course assignment, University of Maryland, 2006.
24. Deighton, "How."
25. "Quaker," p. D10.
26. "Shareholders," p. 6.
27. "Snapple Buyout," p. 13.
28. "Quaker," p. D10.
29. Harbour, " Five."
30. Ibid.
31. Coca-Cola Bottling Co.
32. Pepsico Inc.
33. Feder, "Quaker," p. D1.
34. "Triarc Annual Report."
35. Ibid.
36. Bradsher, "Nynex," p. D1.
37. Verhovek, "New York," p. B3.
38. Campbell-Smith, "The New," p. S1.
39. "Number," p. D7.
40. Bradsher, "Nynex," p. D1.
41. Campbell-Smith, "The New," p. S1.
42. "Mobile," p. 65.
43. Ramirez, "Company," p. D4.
44. Campbell-Smith, "The New," p. S1.
45. Urlocker, "Digital," p. 3.
46. Young, "Wireless."
47. "Tough," p. 47.
48. Greenstein, "The Anatomy."
49. Young, "Wireless."

Bibliography

Adler, Stella. *The Technique of Acting*. New York: Bentham Book, 1988.

Bossidy, Larry, and Ram Charan, *Confronting Reality*. New York: Crown Publishing, 2004.

Bradsher, Keith. "Nynex Plans Pedestrian's Mobile Phone." *New York Times*, August 2, 1990: D1.

"Business: Consultant, Heal Thyself; Management Consulting." *The Economist, Volume 365, Issue 8297*, November 2, 2002: 73.

Camerer, Colin, F., George Loewenstein, and Drazen Prelec. "Neuroeconomics: How Neuroscience Can Inform Economics." *The Journal of Economic Literature, XLIII (March 2005)*: 9–64. Reproduced in Maital, Shlomo (Ed.), *Recent Development in Behavioral Economics* (Elgar Publishing, 2007).

Campbell-Smith, Duncan. "The New Boys: A Survey of Telecommunications." *The Economist, Volume 321, Issue 7727*, October 5, 1991: S1.

Carter, Rita. *Mapping the Mind*. Berkeley, Calif.: University of California Press, 1999.

Coca-Cola Bottling Co., SEC 10k-filing, 1998. *sec.edgar-online.com/1998/03/27/10/0000950168-98-000895/Section8.asp*. Accessed July 2008.

Cubbin, John, and Paul A. Geroski, "The Convergence of Profits in the Long Run." *Journal of Industrial Economics*, 35 (4) (1987): 427–41.

Dana, Jason, and George Loewenstein. "A Psychological Perspective on the Influence of Gifts to Physicians From Industry." *Journal of the American Medical Association*, 290 (2) (2003):252–5.

Davis, L. J. "Television's Real-Life Cable Baron." *New York Times*, December 2, 1990.

Deighton, John. "How a Juicy Brand Came Back to Life." *Harvard Business School*, February 4, 2002. *hbswk.hbs.edu/item/2752.html*. Accessed July 2008.

Deutschman, Alan. "Sly as Fox." *New York Times Magazine*, October 18, 1998.

Fabrikant, Geraldine. "Broadcasters Bet on Sports As First Step In New Markets." *New York Times*, March 4, 1996.

Feder, Barnaby J. "Quaker to Sell Snapple for $300 Million." *New York Times*, March 28, 1997.

"Fox/Liberty Buys Madison Square Garden Stake." *Financial Post*, Volume 10(80)(June 24, 1997): 16.

"GE Chief Sees Growth Opportunities in 2008." *USA Today*. December 14, 2007.

Greenstein, Shane. "The Anatomy of a Foresight Trap." *IEEE Micro*, June 2005. Accessed through *www.kellogg.northwestern.edu/faculty/greenstein/images/htm/Columns/anatomy.pdf*. Accessed July 2008.

Hallowell, Edward M. "Overloaded Circuits: Why Smart People Underperform." *Harvard Business Review*, January 1, 2005.

Harbour, Steven E. (May 15, 1997) "Five Rules of Distribution Management." *Business Horizons*, May 15, 1997. *findarticles.com/p/articles/mi_m1038/is_n3_v40/ai_20141976*. Accessed July 2008.

Hill, Michael E. "Fans Wonder Where the Big Fans Will Be When NFL leaves CBS." *The Gazette*, January 29, 1994.

Jones, Del. "It Is Lonely and Thin-Skinned at the Top." *USA Today*, January 16, 2007: 1B–2B.

Kahneman, Daniel. "A Perspective on Judgment and Choice." *American Psychologist*, 58, September 2003: 697–720.

Kirzner, Israel M. *Perception, Opportunity and Profit*. Chicago: University of Chicago Press, 1979.

Kissel, Howard (Ed.). *Stella Adler: The Art of Acting*. New York: Applause, 2000.

Koch, H.W. *A History of Prussia*. New York: Barnes & Noble Books, 1978.

Lesly, Elizabeth. "Cablevision Loses Its Tunnel Vision." *Business Week*, October 20, 1997. *www.businessweek.com/1997/42/b3549097.htm*. Accessed July 2008.

"Little Wars and Kreigspiel." Appendix to H.G. Wells's *Little Wars*. On the Gutenberg Project Website. *www.gutenberg.org/dirs/etext03/ltwars11.txt*. Accessed January 2008.

Lowry, Tom. "ESPN's Full-Court Press." *Business Week*, February 11, 2002. *www.businessweek.com/magazine/content/02_06/b3769071.htm*. Accessed July 2008.

McGirt, Ellen. "Getting Out From Under." *Fortune*, March 20, 2006.

Milicia, Joe. "Web Presents New Rivals for Ticketmaster." *USA Today* (Web edition), "Money" section. January 18, 2008. *www.usatoday.com/tech/products/services/2008-01-18-ticketmaster_n.htm*. Accessed January 2008.

"Mobile Telephones: Digital Daze." *The Economist*, October 3, 1992: 65.

"Number of Cellular Users Is up 40%, Industry Reports." *New York Times*, March 18, 1992: D7.

Oster, Sharon M. *Modern Competitive Analysis*. New York: Oxford University Press, 1994.

"Out Foxed." *Sports Illustrated* Volume 79(26)(December 27, 1993): 16.

Pepsico Inc., SEC 10-Q filing, 1998. *sec.edgar-online.com/1998/07/28/11/0000077476-98-000035/Section9.asp*. Accessed July 2008.

Porter, Michael E. *Competitive Strategy*. New York: The Free Press, 1980.

"Quaker Oats Buys Snapple; Shareholders Sue Over Price." *Toronto Star*, November 3, 1994: D10.

Ramirez, Anthony. "Company News: Cellular Telephone Industry Counts 11 Million Customers." *New York Times*, March 3, 1993, Late Edition (East Coast).

Rose, Frank. "There's No Business Like Show Business. In Fact, It Just May Be the Weirdest Business on Earth." *Fortune*, June 22, 1998. *money.cnn.com/magazines/fortune/fortune_archive/1998/06/22/244178/index.htm*. Accessed July 2008.

Rosenzweig, Phil. *The Halo Effect*. New York: Free Press, 2007.

Rotte, Joanna. *Acting with Adler*. New York: Limelight Editions, 2000.

Sandomir, Richard. "Broadcast Giants Vie for Control of Regional Sports Markets." *New York Times*, September 1, 1997.

——. "Cablevision Locks Up Garden." *New York Times*, February 23, 2005.

"Shareholders Upset as Quaker Buys Snapple." *Financial Post*, November 3, 1994: 6.

Sidel, Robin. "Broader Troubles in Citi Shakeup." *Wall Street Journal*, November 5, 2007. Quoted in *www.mindfully.org/Industry/2007/Citi-$11B-Charges5nov07.htm*. Accessed January 2008.

"Snapple Buyout Rumors Fly but Gig Guns Mum." *Financial Post*, October 22, 1994: 13.

"State of Competition in the Cable Television Industry." September 24, 1997, House of Representatives, Committee on the Judiciary, Washington, D.C. Accessed through *commdocs.house.gov/committees/judiciary/hju47850.000/hju47850_0.HTM#FR23*. Accessed July 2008.

"Tough at the Top." *The Economist, Volume 338, Issue 7947*, January 6, 1996: 47.

Triarc Annual Report 1997. *media.corporate-ir.net/media_files/irol/67/67548/pdfs/1997_Triarc_Annual_Report.pdf*. Accessed July 2008.

Tully, Shaun. "In this corner! The contender!," *Fortune*, March 29, 2006. Online edition accessed through *money.cnn.com/magazines/fortune/fortune_archive/2006/04/03/8373068/index.htm*. Accessed January 2008.

Turner, Dan. "Fox Accuses Disney, Cable Firms of Blocking its New Sports Channel." *Los Angeles Business Journal*, March 10, 1997. *findarticles.com/p/articles/mi_m5072/isn_10_v19/ai_19490951*. Accessed July 2008.

Urlocker, Mike. "Digital Network to Cost $100M." *Financial Post, Volume 5, Issue 12* February 21, 1992: 3.

Verhovek, Sam Howe. "New York Telephone Has the Bronx's Number, and It's 718." *New York Times*, Late Edition (East Coast), December 11, 1990: B3.

Vranica, Suzanne. "NBC, ESPN Bang Helmets as TV Football Nights Shift." *Wall Street Journal*, July 31, 2006. *www.post-gazette.com/pg/06213/710214-66.stm*. Accessed July 2008.

Weber, Joseph. "J.P. Morgan Is in for a Shock." *Business Week*, February 2, 2004. *www.businessweek.com/magazine/content/04_05/b3868084_mz020.htm*. Accessed January 2008.

Wells, H.G. *Little Wars*. London: F. Palmer, 1913.

——. *Floor Games*. London: F. Palmer, 1911.

Woodyard, Chris. "Car Sales Lowest in Almost 10 Years." *USA Today*, January 4, 2008: 1B.

Yahoo! Finance. Accessed July 2006.

Young, Jeffery S. "Wireless Wonderland." *Forbes*, March 25, 1999. *www.forbes.com/1999/03/25/feat.html*. Accessed July 2008.

Index

D

E

F

G

N

O

P

R

S

About the Author

For two decades, **Benjamin Gilad** has been running war games for market-leading Fortune 500 firms in a variety of industries, and on six continents. He is a former associate professor of strategy at Rutgers University's School of Management, and the founder and president of The Academy of Competitive Intelligence. A pioneer of competitive intelligence (CI) theory and practice in the United States, he was called "our CI guru" by the Society of Competitive Intelligence Professionals. He holds a PhD in economics, an MBA, and a BA in psychology and philosophy. He lives in Boca Raton, Florida.